TOTAL
LIFE
MANAGEMENT

Bob Shank

MULTNOMAH

Portland, Oregon 97266

All Scripture references are from the Holy Bible: New International Version, copyright 1973, 1978, 1984 by the International Bible Society. Used by permission of Zondervan Bible Publishers.

Edited by Al Janssen
Cover design and illustration by Durand Demlow

TOTAL LIFE MANAGEMENT
© 1990 by Robert R. Shank
Published by Multnomah Press
Portland, Oregon 97266

Multnomah Press is a ministry of Multnomah School of the Bible, 8435 Northeast Glisan Street, Portland, Oregon, 97220

Printed in the United States of America

Library of Congress Cataloging-in-Publication Data

Shank, Bob.
 Total life management : who needs it, what you gain with it, why you lose without it, how to achieve it / by Bob Shank.
  p.   cm.
 ISBN 0-88070-360-1
  1. Success—Religious aspects—Christianity. 2. Time management—Religious aspects—Christianity. 3. Christian life—1960-   I. Title.
 BV4598.3.S5 1990
 248.4—dc20   90-36851
                                                                  CIP

90 91 92 93 - 4 3 2 1

Dedication

To Cheri, my partner in life and purpose

"Make my joy complete
by being like-minded, having the same love,
being one in spirit and purpose."

Paul of Tarsus
Philippians 2:2

Contents

Foreword

Most people spend more time planning for Christmas or for their vacation than planning for their entire life!

I am convinced that every person—that *you*— has the potential for a life mission that is truly unique. It emerges from what you find naturally satisfying and fulfilling. Within that mission, your personal definition of success and significance will be unique and different from that of every other person.

Gaining this kind of focus—a sense of purpose for living—is a process. It involves working out and developing a strategic plan. The benefit you can expect to derive makes the process worthwhile: With a clear statement of purpose, you will move steadily with confidence toward that which is personally fulfilling.

In this book, Bob Shank has addressed this process succinctly and simply. He argues passionately for the preparation of a life-purpose statement, gives you the practical steps to build your own, and presents the life example of Jesus of Nazareth as the greatest mission-driven figure in history. Your future could be transformed by adopting the principles you will discover in the pages of this book.

Those who have a mission—a purpose—for life possess the key to living a meaningful life. Will you be a mission driven person?

DENIS WAITLEY

Acknowledgments

All of us live under the influence of the Law of Limited Resources: The time invested in any project is taken from some other place in one's life. The time I invested in the preparation of this manuscript was made available for this purpose by some understanding people.

One group who made it possible is my family. To my wife, Cheri, and my two dynamite daughters, Shannon and Erin, I offer my gratitude. Your willingness to release the time required from me to finish this project was no small sacrifice.

Another important group who gave of themselves is my staff at Priority Living. For your indulgences toward me during the weeks when "the book" moved in front of your issues on my priority list, my heartfelt thanks. You've made this book possible through your personal commitments.

Last, two great editorial partners have helped to clarify and organize the finished product. To Al Janssen and Steve Halliday belong a laurel wreath of recognition. They are a part of a great team who have honored me by publishing this book through Multnomah Press. You are great partners to have in such an enterprise!

CHAPTER ONE

Goal Overload

If there's one thing Americans are good at, it's maximizing their career potential.

If there's one thing Americans struggle with, it's maximizing their life potential.

The man across the hotel restaurant breakfast table was a picture of success. Brad had built his company over the last fifteen years into a recognized leader in the high-tech industry he helped to pioneer. He arrived that morning in a new European sedan that sported dual cellular phone antennas on the rear windshield. Our mutual friend who had arranged this meeting had briefed me enough to let me know that Brad was a locally famous guy with some big-time hurts.

As he lightly buttered his bagel, Brad unfolded for me the story of his professional rise. Born to be a maker of deals, his current job description no longer contained the things that made his work fun. The tedium of managing an organization had replaced the thrill of the hunt, and he didn't like it. He shook his head as he told me about a corporate entity that had become a burden instead of a prize.

Things weren't much better on the home front. His marriage was showing signs of wear. A wife who met the tests of compatibility years before, now little resembled the beach-loving girl he married. Three active kids defined her life today, and Brad wasn't there nearly enough to pull what she thought was his part of the load. He had given them all the goodies, but they weren't squealing with satisfaction.

"Guys with stress at work and stress at home need a break," Brad told me. He described a group of buddies who shared his frustration with the price of life in the fast lane. Their incomes allowed regular escapes, which had conveniently become men-only by definition. They were tired all-stars in search of a respite, but my new friend told me it wasn't working.

Two things had precipitated Brad's agreeing to meet with me. One was an opportunity to expand his business into its next phase of growth . . . but it was a move that would put him in airports and hotel rooms every week for the next five years. Dynamic growth has its price, and Brad was going to have to pay if he decided to answer this opportunity's knock. Was he willing to ante up? Would his family buy in, or blow out?

The other situation was a heart problem known only to him. Not the physical variety, but the romantic kind. A consultant employed by his corporation was helping him update a business plan for the expansion, and their professional relationship was beginning to assume a different tone. Brad was feeling the tug of the hormones.

The consultant, a competent MBA from a major West Coast university, was the best he had ever met in her field. Young, confident, and in tune with the contemporary corporate culture, she had plugged into his mind on a frequency his wife had never been able to attain. Though nothing had happened yet, he knew that it was only a matter of time before one thing led to another.

A distant backdrop to this nightmare was a sense of moral responsibility that nagged at him relentlessly. As a college student, Brad told me, someone had confronted him with the historic Christian faith. After weeks of exploring his "What about?" questions and enjoying the company of a campus fellowship of Christians, he had decided to join them in their relationship with God.

He still acknowledged his faith, albeit nominally, through a socially acceptable church in the community. But his convictions hadn't offered any earthshaking solutions to his confusion. They had only served to unsettle him as he watched the options exercised by his peers. A number of his friends had abandoned any beliefs or constraints that inhibited their freedom for self-serving, mid-life revolution. "I know that some of the things I'm considering aren't the best," he told me. "But I find myself entertaining them anyway."

Life wasn't fun anymore for Brad. The price required for success was no longer a good deal. His friends who had made radical moves in response to the same hopeless emotions were bigger basket cases afterwards than they were before. Brad was sincere: he wanted to know what to do.

What do you say to a guy who has achieved all of his goals and now wants to know why it feels so empty?

The Great American Nightmare

This wasn't the first time I'd heard such a combination of woes from a person whose life seemed to be the picture of success. America seems to be growing a bumper crop of men and women who find themselves winning in business and losing in life. Trained as technicians, prepared to spin the dials and work the system, they've got the machine spitting out big checks with their names on them—but the thrill is gone.

There are a lot of people doing very well today between 8:00 and 5:00. You may see their pictures in the business section of the *Los Angeles Times*, announcing their most recent promotion. Probably they have been featured in some industry-wide publication that heralds them as one of the up-and-comers in their specialty. They are the folks asked to lead the workshops and seminars.

Then there comes a traumatic moment when they have to leave the office and reenter real life. The prominence they enjoyed in the marketplace is about to be replaced by an intense sense of dysfunction. Their contemporaries tell them they are successful, but privately they admit their capability ends at the business door.

It is possible to win at business but lose at life. It happens every day to people you know. It may even be happening to you.

It certainly was happening to Brad. Just imagine: a guy with an earned doctorate, great company, six-figure income, cute wife, healthy kids, a gymnast's physique . . . and miserable. Only in America! He wouldn't evoke much sympathy from most people who view him as a model for their own lives instead of a victim of the system.

It was my turn to talk. With my breakfast growing cold, the conversation began to warm up. I told Brad I understood how he felt. It had been nearly ten years before, but I could still remember asking the same kinds of questions and feeling similar emotions. I colored for him a picture of my public accomplishment and private concern.

After being out of school for a decade, I had blitzed some of the big decisions of life and gotten lucky, or so it seemed. The company I joined in 1970 had become the focus of my career. A privately held corporation, it dominated its field in our part of the state. I had taken over the operation from the owner to allow for his semi-retirement. My title was "executive vice-president," but I got to run the firm like it was my own. Business had more than tripled in the four years I had been responsible. I had assembled a great management team, and they were humming.

With nearly three hundred employees, innumerable clients, and attentive vendors, I never lacked for someone who wanted a piece of my time. The protocol of leadership carried certain personal responsibilities. Relationships founded on the working environment ate up mealtimes and social opportunities.

Visibility in the industry also meant giving something back. Volunteer service on standards committees and professional associations was sometimes a nuisance, but it was junk food for the ego. I was developing an impressive multi-page résumé.

Cheri and I had been married for nearly a decade by then. Two daughters under age seven kept her occupied, while I pursued my own agenda away from home. A succession of high-demand hobbies occupied all the time I could spare. Distance running with quarterly marathon competitions and private white-water rafting adventures on western rivers consumed my attention during hours away from work.

I related to Brad's spiritual heritage as well. A Christian since my youth, I found satisfaction participating in a variety of ways with our local church, as well as through some Christian business organizations. In fact, some of my deepest fulfillment came from the people I knew in these capacities. It felt good when dormant feelings of selfless service began to surface.

You don't do all of that without managing your time well. Cheri and I were masters at cramming activity into compact schedules. Friends were in awe of our itinerary. "I don't know how the two of you do it," won the prize for most-expressed comment by guests around our dinner table.

If you looked up *goal-oriented* in an encyclopedia, I think you would have found our pictures in the margin. We were setting up goals and clicking them off. If you could mount goals when you fulfilled them, our family room would have been lined with trophies. Boy, could we pursue goals.

As for my wife, the stories of her roommother roles, her service as field-trip concierge at the kids' private school, her leadership of a women's organization, numbered in the hundreds. The recitation of her meritorious deeds were matched by my tales of business deals and weekend expeditions "where no man had gone before."

But we were disaster in the making. "Ships passing in the night" sounded like a colorful exaggeration when she would say it, but Cheri was right. We were greeting each other's vapor trails as we came and went every day. Something had to give.

A Time for Reappraisal

The nagging sense of deficiency finally gave birth to a summit conference. It was the fall of the year, and Cheri and I had hit the end of our ropes. I booked a weekend in Palm Springs, called home, and announced the challenge: "We're going away for the weekend to make some sense out of this life we've got out of control. And we're not coming back until we have an answer!"

At this juncture, my breakfast buddy was leaning forward into the story. I could see him spotting the similarities in our lives. The "Nobody's been through this and lived!" look was fading from his face. "What happened?" he interrupted. "What did you do when you got to Palm Springs?"

I told him what Cheri and I did that weekend, and how it literally changed our lives. Our crisis made us analyze the problem and it forced us to find some permanent solutions. In time, we began telling others what we'd learned, particularly one eye-opening truth. We've watched this principle bring order and direction to people who had most everything they thought they wanted from life—except contentment.

The more we were able to help others, the more my business career began to fade in importance. Eventually I left my "perfect" job to spend full time helping people achieve significance after they recognize there is more to life than just "success."

Significance and balanced life-management are not elusive dreams. Over a period of several weeks I was able to guide Brad through a few basic exercises that produced a new game plan for his life. This time it was balanced. Some of the changes were hard to implement emotionally, but Brad persevered, and the renewed love for his life, his family, and his business were the benefits that motivated him to make these changes permanent.

You, too, can bring order and balance to your frantic existence. The spark *can* be renewed in a fading marriage. There *is* a reason for life that goes beyond the next big deal. You *can* discover how to sort through the confusing and conflicting demands of people and projects. If you feel locked inside a maze, *there is an escape.*

I invite you to invest just a few hours exploring the principles in this book. If you do, I promise you will discover a fresh outlook on life. And if you take some time to do the suggested **Life Management** exercises, you will find yourself in control of your future.

Total Life Management is not a dream. It's a real possibility. It begins by addressing a fundamental prerequisite. Fulfill this and you'll unlock a secret most people never discover; a secret that opens the doors to Total Life Management.

CHAPTER TWO

The Missing Prerequisite

The silver-haired man walks onto the stadium field and stops the groundsman raking the cinders on the third-base path. "Looks like the doubleheader won't be a sellout," he says to the workman. "Best seats in the place are still in the dugout," comes the reply.

The distinguished-looking stranger heads to the dugout under the empty stands, making a visible path through the morning dew on the infield grass. He reaches into the bat rack, pulls out a manila envelope, and sits down on the bench. He removes a small tape player from the envelope and finds a cued reel of audio tape. He turns on the machine as he opens a smaller envelope that has been packed with the tape recorder. Out of it falls several black-and-white glossies.

"Good morning, Mr. Phelps. The man with the turban is the Omar of Lasagna. His leadership has been threatened by a radical group headed by Abra Cadabra, shown here with his two wives. If Cadabra and his Front for the Liberation of Lasagna are successful, it will mean the destabilization of the entire region. Your mission, Jim, if you choose to accept it, is to neutralize the opposition to the Omar's administration and assure the peace of Lasagna. As always, Jim, if you or any member of your IM team are apprehended, the secretary will disavow any knowledge of your actions. Good luck, Jim." A hiss and then a plume of smoke follows the recorded message as the tape self-destructs.

Millions have watched Peter Graves accept his Mission: Impossible week after week, confident of his willingness to tackle the most incredible challenges. The television screen never goes blank during prime time because he decides not to accept the mission. And there is never any question about the outcome. It's fascinating to discover the details of his operating plan, but you can always count on the results. The mission is always accomplished.

Week in and week out, the IM Force has a mission statement that directs its activities. This fictional team knows what fits and what doesn't, based on its contribution to the fulfillment of the mission. The members' ability to order their lives while engaged in the mission is consistent and deliberate.

Could it be that our lives often end in tragedy because we lack the same kind of focus?

This is a book with a mission. The purpose of this book is:

1) to help you see the immense importance of defining a mission statement for your life;

2) to help you formulate a personal life-mission statement;

3) to show you how to go about managing your life in keeping with your mission.

Goals Aren't Enough

Let me tell you from the onset that this is not another book about setting goals. I have read books, attended seminars, and invested weeks of my adult life in service to goals. Sadly, most of that time has produced more frustration than fruit. Let me explain.

One seminar directed me to break my life into bite-sized nuggets; every dimension that demanded time and energy deserved a separate goal. I made the typical list:

- Professional
- Marriage
- Family
- Financial
- Spiritual
- Physical
- Educational
- Charitable
- Recreational

Your list may vary some, but everyone's list is similar. I learned how to explore each of these areas in order to construct clear, measurable goals for each one. My life, I was told, was going to be enhanced by my ability to see personal progress in each of these important facets of my life.

If you had dropped in on my life ten years ago, you would have found my goals clearly defined. I knew where I was going in each of these dissimilar areas. I was on my way.

Managing my time became a function of advancing my goals. That's when some of my problems set in. Seems that some of my goals weren't getting along with one another. That's putting it mildly; truth was, some of them were fighting like cats and dogs.

Goals at War

Let me illustrate. Take three of the things I was pursuing:

- *Professionally*, we were trying to increase our profits in the midst of a shrinking market. That meant I needed to spend more time at the office shaving expenses and increasing margins through better quality contracts with clients who needed to see me personally. If my professional goals were to be realized, I needed to invest myself.

- *Physically*, I was trying to reduce my marathon times. My training schedule had me running about fifty miles a week. That needed to go up to seventy. I needed to find another four hours a week to devote to training if I was going to achieve my objective.

- *Personally,* I was committed to spending more time with my daughters, who were increasingly aware of my absence and knew enough to ask where I was. If they were going to be impressed with their dad and view me the way I wanted to be viewed, they needed more time with me. I couldn't delegate this project to anyone else: these were my babies.

There you have it. Three bona fide arenas of life. Three simple, understandable goals. No glaring problems with these, right? Wrong!

Stay at the office just one more hour each day. Arrive home at 6:00 instead of 5:00. Sprint up the stairs, suit up in your Nikes and windsuit for the last rays of daylight, and hit the streets. Stretch your daily hour training run by a half hour to get the mileage base up. Sail back home, dripping and in need of a cool-down period, to the sight of the family around the dining room table, waiting for dinner to convene ninety minutes later than it used to. Wolf down your chow, try to stimulate meaningful small talk with the tiring troops, and then pack the midgets off to bed by their 8:30 bedtime.

Oh, the joys of the goal-oriented life! Have you ever debated the merits of your plans for career enrichment or your invigorated exercise program when faced with a life partner who wants to know where she and your progeny fit in?

And that's only three of the areas! There was more to it for me, as there is for you. The more complex your life mix, the more bizarre the potential problems. I had defined numerous areas of my life that qualified for designated, defined goals. Talk about tension: I couldn't pursue a single one of the goals without feeling competition from others at the same moment.

So where are you feeling the tension?

- You may feel it in your compulsion to "pay your dues" at the office by working far into the night until you get the promotion.

- You may notice it most when you fall asleep over the textbooks for the class you've got to finish this semester to get your degree in June.

- You may experience it when you're waiting for a six-year-old to spit out a story over breakfast while you're waiting to leave for an important meeting.

- You may discover it lurking alongside you as you sleep in with your spouse on Sunday while feeling guilty about not being at church where your mom said you belonged.

My goals, originally intended to increase my satisfaction with life, were traumatizing me. Each of them called for my attention, making a rational case for priority in my schedule.

Achievement even began to betray me. Goals, once accomplished, simply put me on new ground from which to view the next, higher range. Closure gave way to expanded demands. My goals had become gremlins that were fighting with one another and gnawing on my mind. Obviously, my goals needed to be synthesized, but that wasn't part of the training!

Which goals really fit in my life? How could I pursue these positive promises of a bright future and select the right combinations that would get along with one another?

I discovered the answer in the formulation of a life-purpose statement.

The Foundation for Goals

During our summit conference in Palm Springs, Cheri and I spent the bulk of two days exploring the answers to three questions:

1. What unique gifts, resources, and talents did we bring to our marriage? What were the things we could do better than anything else?

2. What had we learned about our natural personal tendencies? How did we work best with one another and with other people? In what environments were we most effective?

3. For what did we have a heart? If we could change any single thing in the world through investing our lives in the cause, what would it be?

As best we knew how, we tried to give substance to these intangibles. The time spent discussing and debating these points allowed us to arrive at a consensus by the time we were finished.

We looked like superpowers trying to agree on a disarmament proposal, but we finally gave birth to a statement we both could own. No one snapped any pictures or played a blast of bugles, but it was in that hotel room that we first crafted a document we have since come to value as a personal treasure.

It's important to understand exactly what we were doing. We were laying a foundation that would allow us to set realistic goals. The goals came later in the process; they were not the guiding force.

I had always started with goals rather than ending with them. I had been taught to ask, "What are your goals?" rather than, "What is your purpose?" Here are the elements we found we needed:

- A ***purpose*** statement that takes into account how we're qualified, where we're effective, and where our passion directs us for the whole of our lives . . . all of what we are, for as long as we are. This gives us a reason for the things we do and the lives we live.

- A ***vision*** of our future that projects our direction as we pursue our purpose. This meets our need to see past today and to see how we are progressing.

- A sense of ***mission*** that motivates even the mundane aspects of life, allowing us to see how all things fit into the bigger picture. Mission is your purpose in action.

- A challenge of ***strategy*** that sharpens our thinking as we constantly assess the resources at hand and opportunities available to us. This allows us to manage ourselves and our self-investments in keeping with our life plan.

- A reasonable set of ***goals*** that harmonize rather than clash with one another. These goals make it possible to choose the best areas to invest ourselves, and to bypass anything less.

Living on Purpose

When's the last time someone looked you square in the eye and asked you to articulate your purpose statement? If you were asked to do that today, how would you answer?

Goals and purpose are apples and oranges. By my independent survey, over 80 percent of the people willing to answer the question, "What is your life purpose?" gave me a goal rather than a purpose.

One man answered, "My purpose is to retire and travel." That is not a purpose; that is a goal.

Another man said, "My purpose is to be a good husband and father." Great goal, but not a purpose.

From a woman I interviewed: "My purpose is to be the first woman on the board of [organization]." She did it; it was a goal.

So what's the difference?

A **goal** is always measurable, accomplishable within a given period of time, and will be replaced by a new goal once achieved. You can have multiple goals at any given time.

A **purpose** is not measurable, is never fully attainable in this life, and will only be refined and restated (never replaced) in your lifetime—if it is the right purpose for you. You will only have one purpose active in your life.

Did you realize that the quality and extent of your life depend, to some degree, on your ability to define your purpose and mission in life?

How would you answer the question "What is your life purpose?" Is there a manila envelope waiting somewhere for you? What would be on the tape when you hear, "Your mission, should you choose to accept it, is _____"?

If you know the answer to that question, you're already ahead of most people. However, don't be discouraged if you can't answer it. I'm going to provide you with a step-by-step plan to help you arrive at your own personal life-purpose statement.

CHAPTER THREE

The Value
of Purpose

He inherited his position from his father, who recognized potential in him through early successes. The son was encouraged to use his exceptional abilities to blow out the boundaries and take the operation far beyond the confines that existed when he took over.

At age twenty he became CEO. Within a few years, his vision and innovation directed the troops to new victories and expansive growth. By the time he reached thirty, he controlled the market. He was a goal-oriented leader of the first degree. His name was on everything. He was the model of success. So successful that he lacked any more worlds to conquer.

Major error: Call your goals your reason for living and then achieve them all. Result: Lose your reason for living.

When that happened to Alexander the Great, history records that he sat down, placed his head in his hands, and wept. He met all of his objectives and had nowhere else to go. Soon he grew despondent, his drinking went out of control, and he stopped achieving. Three years later, at age thirty-three, he was dead.

Abraham Maslow is remembered for his insights into human psychology. One of Maslow's most fascinating pursuits was his research on the effects of purpose in people's lives. He concluded that both the quality and quantity of life were affected by a person's intensity of purpose. In fact, the length of one's life is directly linked to his or her sense of purpose felt at mid-life. In Maslow's observations, if you didn't possess a reason big enough to define your life, you wouldn't live as long as someone who did.

Inadequate Substitutes

In contemporary American society, most people derive their purpose from their activities, rather than deriving their activities from their purpose. *You **are** because of what you **do***, they think. That's backwards!

Career-driven men and women who don't consciously decide otherwise nearly always attempt to find their purpose in their work. As long as things are going well in their professional lives, they can weather any storm. Life may be in the bucket, but if their last performance review was positive, they would generally gauge their lives successful. Withdraw their title or their business card, and you'll shake their foundations. Impugn their proficiency, and they'll begin to wonder about the value of life. These are the people who jump from windows when their bar charts go south.

Watch the curious dance of people like this when they get their gold watch at retirement. Often, when the dust settles and their effects are removed from their desk, life is over. Aimlessly wandering from hobby to hobby, they struggle to find meaning in life. Otherwise healthy men and women die off in droves just a few years after retirement. But why should that surprise us? They simply don't have a big enough reason to live.

Women who elect to emphasize their children rather than a career are not insulated from this syndrome. Defining their lives by their growing kids, they feel great highs and dramatic lows based on the current status of their offspring. When the kids receive their diplomas and head into adulthood, Mom's success as a parent would seem to be assured. Instead, this often triggers a sense of worthlessness and futility in a home-oriented mom: her reason for existence is now obsolete. If the goal of being a good mom to dependent children was her purpose, she is up for grabs emotionally. Empty nests often lead to strained marriages, mid-life affairs, return to the workplace in search of meaning, and divorce in the forties.

One of the offbeat sights in Los Angeles is the Watts Towers. Built in a neighborhood whose glory has long since passed, they are the life work of a man who couldn't part with a good piece of garbage. Hubcaps, Hula-Hoops, toasters, and tire irons have found their way into this hodgepodge of Americana. If you look closely, you may find a long-discarded piece of your own history. The Watts Towers are simply the result of disparate pieces strained into synthesis. The outcome is curious but worthless.

Any building of value begins with thoughtful design. The intent of the structure and the distinctives of the site combine under the direction of the architect to produce a set of drawings and specifications for the building. Construction elements are chosen in keeping with the plans so that everything comes together to form a truly unique expression of form and function.

Should a life be any less thoughtfully constructed?

A Blueprint for Life

The purpose statement is to life what the architect's model is to the edifice. It gives the rendering, in advance, of the final product as expressed by the designer. A blueprint follows, in which every goal and activity is chosen in keeping with how it will contribute to the overall scheme.

Imagine calling subcontractors and workmen to converge on a construction site with no architectural plans! The finest carpentry job will be meaningless if it is not integrated with every other element of the process. Excellence in the details will be devoid of importance if the finished composite is valueless.

Great buildings are not so designated because of the quality of their parts, but because of how those quality pieces fit together in harmony and precision. Great plans are more important than great pieces. In fact, average elements can combine to become magnificent cathedrals!

Here's an interesting exercise: get a pencil and jot down six of the greatest names of history. (Let me prime your pump: Thomas Edison, Clara Barton, Shakespeare, Joan of Arc, Lincoln, Luther, Galileo, King. Get the picture?)

Got a list? Let me ask you a question or two about your names. What one thing distinguishes them for the list? What do you know of their incomes? How about their material possessions? Can you tell me their hobbies or recreational preferences?

Chances are, the names on your list are all known for a singular cause or contribution they made to civilization. I doubt there were any "generalists" on your list—people who did a lot of things in an above-average way, but did nothing exceptional. I suspect that most of them were single-minded, driven, sold-out to a particular end for which they gave their all. With regard to their holdings and financial accomplishments, chances are you would have to bury yourself in a library to get a fuzzy answer.

> *The great men and women of history were not great because of what they owned or earned, but rather for what they gave their lives to accomplish.*

There's one name that belongs on your list, if he isn't there already. Some say he was the most incredible figure of all time. That's really amazing because he lived and died without writing a book, leading an army, fathering a family, or starting a company. He never even traveled beyond the borders of his small country. His name is Jesus of Nazareth.

No life ever demonstrated commitment to purpose more powerfully than Jesus Christ. No life ever demonstrated the compound impact of purpose more than his. No person ever demonstrated the tranquility and peace that attends the purpose-driven approach more than Jesus. The records of his life, written by four men from four different perspectives, display his exquisite expression of purpose and mission in a way that makes perfect sense.

Let me introduce you to the most purpose-driven figure of history.

CHAPTER FOUR

The Mission-Driven Model

If there had been a *Jerusalem Post* two thousand years ago, the Jewish people might well have read stories like these:

Man Turns Wedding into Wine-tasting Party

Mob of 5,000 Pig Out on Boy's Lunch

Walk for Life Reported on Sea of Galilee

Taps Turns to Rap When Boy Crashes His Own Funeral

Blind Beggar Passes Eye test

Back From the Dead: Moses and Elijah Spotted on Mountaintop

Tiny Taxman Finds Religion in a Tree

If we didn't know better, we'd almost think this was the *National Enquirer.*

These weren't isolated incidents. Day after day, crowds were left breathless over the exploits of the man who claimed to be God.

In some ways, he is an unfair example. If the statements attributed to Jesus and his followers are true, he is not like you and me. Jesus wasn't just an ordinary guy; he was the eternal God, born into the race through a young virgin supernaturally impregnated by God. He was a never-to-be-repeated phenomenon—the Son of God.

He also planned, however, to be an example. He is presented as the model of what God intended our lives to be. Jesus constantly enjoined people to follow him. His followers encouraged people to follow them as they followed him. He is described as a standard of the first order by which to measure and mold our own lives.

In his deity, he is not duplicable. But in his humanity, Jesus intends to be duplicated!

He did not intend to set a record so astounding that we would not seek to equal it. He intended to leave behind a movement committed to approaching his perfect performance.

Now, I'll be honest with you. I *know* I'll never equal his mark. But that doesn't prevent me from trying.

In 1978 I ran my first marathon. Intending to run just the first half as a training exercise, my buddy John and I felt so good that we went all the way. As we crossed the line together after three hours and thirty-one minutes, we were ecstatic and exhausted.

The next day, I wanted to wear to work the flimsy T-shirt they gave me for finishing the race.

Unfortunately, I couldn't figure out how to get my tie on over it. It seemed like my unsophisticated co-workers had never met a marathon runner. These were the two most asked questions that day:

"You ran a marathon, huh? How long was it?" *What a dumb question! All marathons are the same length—26 miles, 385 yards.*

"Did you win?" *How do you tell someone that the winner crossed the line an hour and twenty minutes before you did, and you feel great about it?*

In ten marathon finishes since then, I haven't crept any closer to the winner's circle, but that hasn't hindered my competitive spirit. I don't expect to win. But I do expect to do better. The winner's performance motivates me, even though I know I will never equal it.

Jesus is the winner who ran the perfect, never-to-be-repeated race. He wears the victor's crown today as he watches me run the course and try for a personal best. His approach to the race is the model for my own. I don't expect to better his time; I just want to better *my* time. No human being can exceed Jesus' accomplishments, but he, as the champion, presents his regimen as a model to increase our capacity.

Have you ever looked at the life of Jesus in that way? Have you delved into the human side of God to find the practical insights he put on record for you and me to maximize our lives? That is what we want to do in this book—to examine the perfect model for life on earth and learn from it.

I realize that discussing Jesus and his relevance produces different emotions for different people. For some the result is reverence; for others it's ridicule.

Perhaps the majority of our world finds itself between those two poles—willing to consider his historic contribution to civilization and culture, but not yet able to relate to him as God in human flesh.

Wherever you find yourself on this continuum, I hope you'll read on. If the most you can accept is that the man Jesus started a movement that went global and has survived nearly twenty centuries, there is still much you can glean from this book. If you regard him as a personal friend and your eternal Savior, you have even more to gain. So don't let his presence scare you. You can learn something from the life of Jesus, no matter where you are.

At the very foundation of the abundant life is this issue of purpose. Jesus knew his purpose on earth. He never made a decision without knowing exactly why he was here and how his actions would affect his mission. Every fragment of his life was in perfect harmony with his purpose. His biographies portray him as occasionally weary, but never frustrated. He never wasted a minute, never pursued a rabbit trail, never went down a blind alley. He was deliberately resolute.

How long must one live to make an impact? Jesus spent thirty years in obscure preparation for his life's work, and then had only three years to exercise his primary emphasis. Could a man really make a difference in such a short time? Jesus felt he could. On the night before his death, he told his father: "I have brought you glory on earth by completing the work you gave me to do."

A life-mission statement that becomes the working blueprint for constructing a life worth remembering—that's what Jesus had. Let's look at what the biblical accounts tell us about his mission.

His mission was determined before his birth

Mary was pregnant and she wasn't married. That's a dilemma in any society. Joseph, her fiancé, wondered what to do, for he knew he wasn't the child's father. In his day, engagement was as binding as marriage and could only be broken through divorce. Being a decent man, Joseph didn't want to expose Mary to public disgrace, so he decided to divorce her quietly.

About this time, an angel appeared to Joseph in a dream. Joseph was told to not be afraid to take Mary as his wife, that her child was conceived by the Holy Spirit. He was instructed to name the child Jesus, "because he will save his people from their sins."

Thirty years passed after the birth of Jesus, and very little is known about those years. In Jewish culture, a man's entry into significance occurred at the age of thirty. Before that, you didn't qualify for important leadership in the community. Jesus was God, yet he fit within the confines of his society. He lived a normal life—so normal that, when he returned to his hometown after beginning his public work, they couldn't believe his miracles. For thirty years he hadn't demonstrated anything supernatural. He was biding his time, preparing for the occasion when his mission would be fulfilled.

It's easy to get fired up about some things in life. It's also fun to be creative and to see yourself as an innovator. We can even dream about founding a new movement or ideology. But where does the impetus come from? Whose idea is it, anyway?

Let me suggest a thought. Jesus stepped into a mission that had been formulated before he arrived on the scene. It existed when he was born. As his adult mind began to function, his mission awaited him. Is the same true of you?

The trick is not to create a purpose, it is to *discover* your purpose. Before you were capable of grappling with the concept, the eternal God had a purpose in mind for you within his over-arching purpose for his world. Like Jesus, your task is not to create a purpose but to embrace the one he already has for you!

His career began with a restatement of his mission

Jesus had a cousin named John, a man whom we know as John the Baptist. John's job was to prepare society for the arrival of the Messiah. He introduced Jesus as that Messiah: "Look, the Lamb of God, who takes away the sin of the world!"

Did you enter your career with a clarity of mission? Did you see how your work fit into your overall direction in life? Or, today, do you find yourself years into a professional pursuit, never having discovered why you do what you do?

Jesus began his career with a restatement of what he was about. Several interesting elements add spice to this story. John is a key person for many reasons:

- He was a mission-driven person himself. His father had received insight from God about John's specific purpose in life: "To go on before the Lord to prepare the way for him, to give his people the knowledge of salvation through the forgiveness of their sins." John accepted this call to be an advance man for the main event, and he was fulfilled within that mission.

- He was entrusted, through divine revelation, with information about Jesus—the knowledge of who Jesus was and what he was sent to do. Listen to what John said:

  ". . . I would not have known him, except the one who sent me to baptize with water told me, 'The man on whom you see the Spirit come down and remain is he who will baptize with the Holy Spirit.' I have seen and I testify that this is the Son of God."

- He understood the mission of Jesus. He wasn't telling Jesus something he didn't already know. His statement was not for Christ's benefit, but for the people standing by and for us today. Jesus didn't "grow into" the shoes of the Messiah, they were designed with him in mind. He didn't decide to become the Son of God on a mission, he was already designated as the Son of God on a mission.

John represents an independent confirmation of Jesus' mission, in much the same way that the Bible today serves to confirm the mission entrusted to people who claim kinship with the Son of God. Your mission is as foundational to your adult life as Jesus' was to him!

His mission defined who he was

Many men and women can only identify themselves in terms of their professions: "I'm a lawyer,"

"I'm president of ABC Corporation," "I sell cars," "I'm an accountant for Abaloney and Zoe." Is your life defined by the label on your business card?

One of the greatest tragedies is to see the identities of men and women stripped away. One moment they're linked with a prestigious company. Then, one Friday afternoon, they're called into an office and told, "We've decided to make some changes." Suddenly they're cleaning out their desks and feeling like nonpersons. They drive home wondering how to announce the news, and where they will go next Monday.

When your identity is connected to your job or to a position in a firm or to your salary, your life is shattered when that connection vanishes. Jesus determined his identity based on his mission. It wasn't based on his being a carpenter for eighteen or so years. His mission defined who he was.

Think about the way you might have handled the kind of treatment that was typical for Jesus. Had he depended on finding himself through the acceptance of others, he would have changed his mission. Had he looked for significance through the gratitude of the people he healed and helped, he never would have found security. If human affirmation had been necessary for him to keep his spirits high, he should have found a different job.

But Jesus found himself in his mission. His willingness to suffer abuse and rejection were based on his understanding of the cost of that mission. Because his identity was found within his pursuit of purpose, he suffered no internal conflict in his circumstances. His security was as well founded as his commitment to his cause.

His mission was not easily understood or quickly embraced

For two years, Jesus made his way around the regions of Judea and Galilee. The masses flocked to him. One big swath of humanity followed his every move.

During this time, he found twelve followers in whom he invested his life. After two years, he began to retreat from the limelight to pour himself into this management team. One day, he asked them a simple question: "Who do people say that I am?"

The disciples listed several options that the masses had suggested for the true identity of Jesus. Then Jesus asked, "Who do *you* say that I am?" Peter answered, "You are the Christ, the Son of the living God."

Bingo! Peter got it right. The disciples were clear where everyone else was fuzzy. So Jesus began to explain why he had come. In restating his mission, he told the disciples that soon he would head up to Jerusalem where he would suffer many things at the hands of the religious leaders. Finally, he would be killed, but three days later he would be raised again to life.

Peter didn't like what he heard, so he pulled Jesus aside. I can just hear Peter telling Jesus off. He probably said something like, "Wait a minute, Jesus! We've got to talk. Do you know what's going to happen if you go through with this? People won't want to follow you. This makes no sense. Just drop it and let's come up with another plan."

Listen: If Peter could treat Jesus like that, don't be surprised if some people are out of step with you over your mission. In fact, some folks will think you are wacko. Some will challenge you over your position. So don't depend on the encouragement of the gallery to continue your quest; support may not be there.

Once you sell out to a life purpose, you also may acquire an enemy who would like to thwart your effectiveness. He is the enemy of all those who live in keeping with God's overall purpose for the planet. His proper name is Lucifer, or Satan. He is often referred to as "the devil." He's a real spiritual personality, firmly opposing all that God plans to do in the cosmos.

The devil was involved in the tiff between Peter and Jesus. Jesus recognized that, and pointed out to Peter that his challenge was stimulated by Satan himself: "Get behind me, Satan! You are a stumbling block to me; you do not have in mind the things of God, but the things of men." Inadvertently, Peter had begun to mouth the message espoused by the other side: The mission wasn't worth the cost!

Jesus is saying, "You are out of step, not me. I'm in step with God; you're in step with men." If you're in step with God, and you have a sense of mission, you will be different from those around you.

Another important thing to remember: Jesus didn't announce his mission to the world. He only revealed it to a select group of people. We might be wise to the do the same.

His commitment to mission increased his impact on people

Jesus headed to Jerusalem knowing it was his final trip on earth. The disciples were astonished that he walked so resolutely to certain death. Again he took the twelve aside and told them what would happen. Still they continued to follow him.

It helps to understand that these disciples were not a rag-tag bunch of transients with nothing better to do. They had jobs. They were in mid-life. They had successful careers. They had investment in capital expenditures essential to their business.

One day years before, Jesus had come along and said, "If you guys are smart, you will walk away from what you're doing and join up with me." He didn't offer them stock options. He didn't offer them management positions. He just said, "Come with me." And they came. Why? He was a magnet personality, and at least part of that magnetism was that he was on a mission. They didn't understand the mission, but they were mightily impressed by it.

We can look at men and women over the course of history and find that those who were on a mission, even a destructive one, drew loyal followers to their cause.

If you want to increase your impact on society, and you want a following of people who can't seem to spend enough time around you—be a person who knows where he is going. You will attract people.

His dedication to mission brought glory to God

I can't get over how Jesus, on the night before he died, said he had completed his mission. So many people I meet never feel they get done with their work. Some feel like they've never even started. When they're near death, they say, "I'm not done; there's so much more I need to do."

But here's Jesus saying he's done after just three-and-a-half years. And he says to God, his father, that this work has brought glory to God. God gets the credit for what was accomplished.

It's tempting to pen a quick purpose statement for your life based on some deeply embedded truth you tucked away in your youth. For many people raised with a religious background, a statement of belief called the Westminster Catechism stands out:

"The chief end of man is to glorify God
and enjoy him forever. . . ."

"Purpose statement?" somebody asks. "Sure, I've got one! My purpose is to glorify God. Simple."

That's good, but it's not enough. Jesus said he had accomplished that end, but he achieved it through a specific means.

Notice what Jesus said. He didn't say that he had glorified God through his belief system. He didn't do it through his faith. He didn't even do it through his tender heart. He said he glorified God by completing the work—the mission—God had given him to do.

This takes it down to a practical level. Jesus didn't just talk a good story—he didn't glorify God in theory. He figured out what God wanted him to do and he did it. I can get my arms around that, can't you?

His mission was completed when his earthly life was over

Hanging on the cross, Jesus uttered these words: "It is finished."

There's a special word for finished. You've experienced it when your desk was clean, the in-basket was empty, and you'd done all that was expected of you. That word is *peace.*

Here's a man on a cross, suffering in agony for your failures in life, bearing the burden of all the combined failure of humankind. And he's at peace!

Why? He was done. His mission was completed.

How would you like to define your target so clearly that you know your mission is complete when you pass away? I submit to you that you'll never be able to say it if you haven't figured out what your purpose is. For what purpose are you here? To move more product? To place more business, write more contracts, employ more people, build bigger buildings, spend more time on the freeway, get bills passed?

For what purpose are you here? The average answers to that question aren't big enough to define life. Yet, I'm just radical enough to believe that every man and woman reading this book has a mission. But for the most part, my observation is that the mission remains undiscovered.

The famous nineteenth-century architect Daniel Burnham, who built America's first skyscraper, once said, "Make no little plans. There's nothing in little plans to stir men's blood. Make big plans. Once a big idea is recorded, it can never die."

Don't define your life in inconsequential terms. It won't carry you very far. If your life is not in line with a grand purpose, there is no good reason to go about it. There is no good reason to answer the bell for the next round when you've been beat up in the last one.

So, what do you do? How do you find your mission in life? If you're interested, Jesus left a great mission. And he has invited you to be a part of it.

CHAPTER FIVE

Your Personal
Mission Statement

By now, I hope you're beginning to get the drift: a personal mission statement is as important to your life as is a set of accurate blueprints to the erection of a quality building. Many lives are under construction without a plan, but the best ones are built with design in mind.

For more than twenty years I have tried one time-management system after another, seeking to bring order to my life. Though they varied in layout and color, a common assumption underlaid all of them: an orderly life results from maintaining orderly days.

Nobody was more faithful than me. My calendar was more likely to accompany me than my wife.

Everything was written down. I was married to my schedule. If a disciplined life was an effective life, I had to be the most effective guy in town.

Wrong! An example of my typical experience:

Ring, ring. "Hello?"

"Hey, Bob? This is Bill. I'd like to talk to you about the cause I mentioned when I ran into you at the club last week. Are you free for lunch on Tuesday?"

I shuffle papers. Reach for the calendar book. Check Tuesday: all clear for lunch. "Yes, Tuesday is free."

"Great! I'll pick you up at your office about noon. I know you'll want to be involved in this thing when you hear about it."

"Are you free?" Are you kidding? Talk about out of control—I was free unless someone else had already nailed me. Sure, I was getting a lot of my own line-items on the calendar. But a huge block of my time was leaking out to other people and their appeals.

On one particularly hectic day, I decided to see how many of my week's activities had been determined by me and how many were scheduled by someone else's request. The answer sobered me immediately. Half of my "optional" time was being scattered to the wind by the control of people who happened to have my phone number.

Clearly, this was unhealthy. Although I never missed an appointment, and my days were ordered with precision—chock full of random activities—my life was out of control.

My working philosophy began to break down. String seven disciplined, disjointed days together into a week, hook fifty-two of these weeks together in succession, and I was supposed to have a meaningful year?

One recent January I lunched with three CEOs. I asked each of them to describe what he considered the most important accomplishment or significant contribution he had made during the prior year. They looked at each other in silence, unable to identify one major achievement from the last twelve months of their lives. They felt the same emotional upheaval I had experienced a few years before.

Here's the confusion:

Well-managed days do not result in a well-managed life. Well-managed days are the result of a well-managed life.

The fact is, you can be disciplined without being deliberate. But God will not hand you a Medal of Honor just for making it to all of your appointments on time.

What follows in the remainder of this chapter is a process to help you formulate a statement of purpose for your life. Your personal statement of purpose can become the foundation for directing how you manage your time, energy, and resources. It is worth whatever it takes you to conceive, carry, and birth it.

Let's use the construction analogy one more time. You are far enough along in life that many elements needed for your mission are already in place. You aren't starting with a bare lot, devoid of construction materials. You're standing on a piece of property, grant deed in hand. Many architectural items already sit in crates on the site, awaiting unpacking and installation. You have a toolbox filled with specific implements. Workmen stand by, expecting direction on how to proceed. It seems you have everything you need to begin—except the plans.

It's up to you to draft the working drawings. However rudimentary they are, it is essential to have something from which to work. It won't suffice to say, "Let's build a house." If no specifics are forthcoming, chaos is only hours away.

A line from *Alice in Wonderland* sure fits here: "If you don't know where you're going, any road will get you there." Even though the pressure's on to get to work, you must take a break and take inventory.

"But what should I draw?" you ask. First, a number of fundamental elements must be surveyed and taken into account. The nature of your piece of property is important: How big is it? Where is it located? What are its characteristics? Your own interests are at issue, too: What kind of house do you want? With what style are you most comfortable? How much space do you need? The materials already gathered require examination: Do they fit together? Are there enough materials to do the job? Do you have working materials that don't belong together?

You also need to sort through the toolbox: What special implements are there? Are the workmen trained to use all of the devices at your disposal? How about the workers: Are they really the right people to build this house? Are there enough? Too many? Will they work together well?

Since you serve as both architect and superintendent, you are keenly interested in creating a good design. In fact, since you'll be living in the place once it's built, you couldn't be more emphatic about the project and its successful completion!

Back to your life: You'll be the one living in it, nobody else. Doesn't it make sense to spend the time necessary to produce the highest quality design possible? I believe God has placed some specific clues around you to assist in the process. In fact, it is his design you want to discover . . . the one that represents his maximum intent for your life. Anything less is to miss the mark of highest and best use.

So let's look at the things unique to you that need to be considered. As we do, use the space provided to write down your observations and ideas. This will provide the information you need to formulate your life-mission statement.

1. Your unique gifts and abilities

One thing that makes you special is the mix of abilities, both natural and spiritual, that have been assigned to you. That's the right word—*assigned*—because God says he chose your gifts and abilities just for you.

Did you ever wish you had someone else's abilities? Did you ever find yourself wondering why you couldn't do what someone else does so well? It's easy to focus on what we can't do in the light of what others can do, forgetting that we have unique capabilities as individual as our fingerprints.

On the natural level we call these abilities *talents*. Some people have an uncanny intellectual capacity that baffles us. Others have the instinct to recognize great investments or business opportunities. In the sports arena, "natural athletes" wow us with their physical prowess. None of these examples can be traced to deliberate, willful choice on the part of the recipient. Someone gave them this potential.

Certainly, two people who have been handed the same talents can come to very different ends, based on their willingness to apply themselves. But the basic, inborn capacity is there through the sovereign decision of the Creator.

When we move to the spiritual arena, people who enjoy a personal relationship with Jesus Christ have received a special gift from God. The Bible calls this a spiritual gift, specifically selected and conveyed by God to members of his family. Broadly speaking, these gifts are either communication gifts or serving gifts. Within those wide parameters are numerous, highly valuable endowments that make participation in the church something vastly better than a dubious exercise in volunteerism. For the enlightened folks who recognize and understand their gifts, service becomes enjoyable and highly effective.

As we move through each element of a complete mission statement, I want to make sure this doesn't become theoretical. So, I will demonstrate by using the process Cheri and I went through as we prepared our purpose statement.

As Cheri and I evaluated what gifts and abilities set us apart, we both recognized that people around us already thought our communication skills were our most identifiable distinctives. Though we could do other things well, we did these things the best.

This was a key piece in our puzzle. Bottom line: We discovered that God could use us to teach other people practical truth about life. Of all of the things we could do in our lives, this was the most rewarding.

Why did God give you unique capabilities? Did he intend you to store them, or to use them center stage? In forging a personal purpose statement, a foundational starting point is determining your gifts and talents. To maximize your life experience you should use these to the fullest extent.

Take some time to think through your natural abilities. List the three which you feel are most likely to play a part in your future:

1)

2)

3)

Now, consider your spiritual gift(s). If you're not sure what your gifts are, read through the following passages, found in the New Testament, and jot down the gifts you think may describe you:

1) Romans 12:3-8:

2) 1 Corinthians 12:1-31:

3) 1 Peter 4:10-11:

2. Your unique personal passion

During the seventies, an innocuous expression became popular: "Whatever turns you on!" People were granted license to pursue anything as long as it

"turned them on." In a misguided way, this encouraged people to pursue their passions, though in
those years passions often went awry.

In the transition from the idealism of the sixties
and early seventies to the hard-line realities of the
eighties and nineties, our generation dropped its passion and forgot to go back and pick it up.

I meet so many people who are living dreary
lives of mere existence rather than energizing lives of
passion. One man told me recently that the strongest
drive that led him out of his marriage was a search
to rediscover some passion for living.

I spent an hour one evening talking with a
young single man struggling to define his purpose.
When I asked about his passion, he immediately
began to relate his deep concern and love for kids
hospitalized with life-threatening illnesses. He told
me how every evening, after work, he spent hours
on the oncology floor of the local children's hospital.
His eyes filled with tears as he recalled name after
name of the boys and girls he befriended during
their struggles with cancer or leukemia.

I asked the man if he hated to go to the children's hospital. He told me he loved it—he hated to
see the kids suffer, but he loved to be there with
them, to comfort them and be a friend.

The years Cheri and I spent in business allowed
us to cultivate and nurture friendships with many
other individuals and couples. Many had gone
through difficult times, and we watched as they
struggled with issues and challenges from which we
had been protected through our faith. We both felt a
burden to help these friends, knowing that help was
available through the faith we shared. Our passion

was to assist men and women within our peer group through the resources of the Christian faith.

Recent surveys of Baby Boomers have probed the question of passion in numerous ways. One survey sought to discover the things that young adults valued enough to be willing to go to war for—in effect, the things for which they would die. The majority did not value a concept, right, or issue enough to risk their lives. Nothing for them was worth dying for.

Here's a thought to ponder: If you don't have anything worth dying for, do you have anything worth living for?

When something so moves your heart and demands your energy that you'd do anything to make it happen, you're onto your passion.

I've discovered something interesting: People driven by passion are so rare and captivating that they tend to draw others to them. They become magnetic and infect others with their passion. People who have never been energized by anything become "kamikazes" for a leader with passion.

Randail Terry, the head of Operation Rescue, has a passion for saving the lives of unborn babies. His passion often has taken him to a jail cell, yet masses surround him, influenced by his passion.

Nelson Mandela, the head of the African National Congress, has a passion for dismantling apartheid in South Africa. His passion held him in a prison cell for decades, yet masses surrounded him, influenced by his passion.

Mother Theresa, the mercy-giver of Calcutta, has a passion for extending kindness in Jesus' name. Her passion keeps her in a place devoid of comfort or ease. Yet masses surround her, influenced by her passion.

The list goes on and on. People with passion will always draw a crowd. They know what they want to see happen, and they're willing to invest everything they have, even their lives.

How about you? Have you cultivated or discovered a passion? Is it planted in your heart and thriving through your life? In the space below, describe the cause or issue that raises your temperature and wins your loyalty:

3. Your unique personality

This is just a guess, but I'll bet you are different from the people closest to you. We all tend to fall into relationships with others whose personalities are significantly different, albeit complementary, from our own.

It is an unusual marriage that finds two similar personalities together. If "we're as different as night and day" were the battle cry for dissolution, 99 percent of marriages would end up on the rocks. Thriving marriages recognize the high odds of big differences, and celebrate them.

You are unique. Your personality is part of your special distinctives, and there are no inherently "bad" personalities. Understanding who you are and how you are inclined is a big piece in the life-management puzzle.

Consider how much this affects your daily activities and your attitude toward them. As a result of your temperament:

- You may enjoy being with people, or you may prefer being alone.

- You may like living with risk, or you may need to feel secure.

- You may enjoy taking leadership, or you may want to follow.

- You may tend to focus on projects, or you may tend to focus on people.

- You may wish to create a movement, or you may look instead for your niche.

None of these differences is right or wrong; they are just different. Hostility and relational stress often erupts when people try to change others into mirror images of themselves. They are often unaware of the foundational differences in individuals, or they think it is a matter of decision, subject to change.

My wife and I conducted a healthy exercise one day while stuck on an airplane with nothing to watch, eat, or hear. I fished through my carry-on bag and found a book given to me by a friend. It was one of the insightful temperament evaluation books on the market. This was the first time that the two of us, together, had a chance to use an objective system to measure ourselves and each other.

What a profitable investment of time! We discovered, much to our amazement, that we are the way we are because that's the way we are. While the descriptions of our temperament types weren't exact expressions of our idiosyncrasies, they were close. Little things that had been big irritants for years were found to be unintentional and inborn. Imagine—she hasn't been doing *that* all these years just to bug me.

For example, in this summary we recognized Cheri as an introvert, while I am clearly an extrovert. That didn't mean she didn't like people, nor that I couldn't stand to be alone. It simply showed that her first choice for elective activity was the exact opposite of mine. She would much prefer to be with family, while I liked to invite a bus load of friends. It would be easy for her to read my tendency as not wanting to be with her and our daughters, when it didn't mean that at all. It was simply an unconscious difference of orientation.

There are numerous resources available to perform just that sort of self-evaluation. The results are valuable in providing a mirror of your temperament.

How does temperament relate to mission? Your statement of mission will not put you in a position outside your constitutional make-up. God made you the way you are for a reason, and he wants to put you to work in a way that takes maximum advantage of your strengths, not in a way that painfully exhibits your weaknesses!

At the risk of sounding ego-driven, many people regard Cheri and me as fun to be with. No one would use the term *sedentary* when referring to us. Those who know me recognize my sense of humor to be a valuable aspect of my make-up. Cheri is more adventurous; she's game to try just about anything. Both of us are comfortable in front of people and want to help them enjoy life a little more. While we have plenty of differences, our personalities are such that we are generally comfortable around people.

Nobody knows you like God does, and he loves the way you're made. Have you discovered the best parts of his design, as seen in your custom personality? If you have a sense of your particular traits, write a paragraph to describe yourself using language that is intangible, rather than tangible (focus on your personality, not your person):

4. Your unique responsibilities

God takes some responsibilities in your life very seriously. You should, too.

I've watched people get fired up about going on a mission to impact the world yet lose the race in the starting blocks. With their hearts set on people across the ocean, whom they've never met, they violate their responsibilities to those they've known for years in their own house.

You carry around a unique set of connections that heaven considers your primary relationships.

- If married, you pack a lifetime linkage to another person. Everything you do has to be considered in light of that person and his or her needs.

- If a parent, you are charged with the task of raising your children to become independent, functioning adults.

- If a child of surviving parents, you carry an obligation to assure the life support of your folks like they did for you.

- If a Christian, you are your brother's keeper to the extent of your capacity to supply his needs from your abundance.

In an era of loosey-goosey lifestyles and flaky commitments, God sounds a somber note of fiduciary and relational responsibility. We are not free to plot our lives on a course that takes us away from the people who depend on us for life support.

This isn't a question of money alone; it includes attention to the emotional, social, and spiritual needs of those in our care. We are to look after the whole person.

During our momentous weekend, Cheri and I reaffirmed our resolute commitment to marriage. Neither of us wrestled with whether we could somehow tank our commitments to one another in favor of some grand mission. Further, we knew that our lifetime impact would rise or fall based on our ability to deliver two healthy daughters to adulthood. Nothing in our life-purpose statement could challenge these priorities for either of us.

Formalize for yourself the names of the people who are your dependents.

Spouse:

Children:

Parents:

Others whom God might consider as
dependent on you:

5. Your unique experiences and education

Nothing is more fun than meeting someone by
chance for the first time and discovering that you
share some common history. Perhaps you were
raised in the same region, or competed against one
another in the same athletic league, or maybe you
attended the same college or university. You may
have known some of the same people, or worked
for the same large corporation during your freshman
career period.

Exploring your similarities with someone is a
fascinating way to begin a relationship, but don't go
overboard. You'll never find anyone who has exactly
the same résumé you have. Even the best of friends,
who commit themselves in their youth to stick
together through thick and thin, get separated. The
winding road of human experience just doesn't seem
wide enough for two to stay together.

As you review the road map of your life, what
do you discover? All of us have spent some time in
backwater experiences we would never want to
repeat, but we carried away mementos that we still
find useful.

The quantity and quality of your education and
experience (I have a hard time separating the two) is

not only a result of where you've been and what you've done, but also how you've invested in where you've been and what you've done. Others could have shadowed you through life until now and arrived destitute.

Although neither Cheri nor I finished college, we both have an extensive list of experiences and accomplishments. We have been able to do things that others deem successful. My years of business and career attainment have won me the right to be heard by people who highly regard such things. Cheri has won the respect of full-time homemakers and professional women alike. Our accomplishments exceed our degrees; we have found we have something to say, and people are willing to listen.

Your education and experience are priceless; you've spent the time since your birth purchasing both. What you are today, and what you have to offer tomorrow are, at least partially, the result of your investments in education and experience.

What are your best assets when you review your background? How are you a better person today as a result of where you've been and what you've done? Often, people don't perceive the value of their experiences until later in life. Time and perspective allow them to discover the truly meaningful moments of their younger years.

Ted has learned this lesson. Many years ago, too-rapid expansion and weak local management forced his multi-state business into involuntary bankruptcy. Although this was a deeply humbling experience for a businessman of high integrity, Ted refused to let this incident blot his background. He doggedly continued to repay the firm's obligations from his personal resources, despite being relieved of personal responsibility by the courts.

Today, Ted has managed to repay every creditor. Moreover, he has used the lessons learned through this experience to deepen his personal resolve and develop his character. His ability to counsel and advise other men and women in similar difficulties is greater today because he made the best of a dreadful situation. He has taken his experience and maximized its value.

Part of the challenge here is to see your credentials in light of the opportunities they offer instead of the restrictions they impose. The "because I studied medicine, I have to be a doctor for the rest of my life" mind-set will give you all of the options of a prisoner on death row (though better paid). Your background is your collection of assets, not a series of chains! If your experiences don't increase your options, you are allowing them to control your future rather than energize it.

Nobody ever will have the exact mix of lessons and life that you bring to the table. You are an expert in the arena touched by your life. How does your expert status in that area increase your capacity for contributing to significant things?

Take a few minutes to reflect on your life experiences. Don't list your alma maters. Think about what you've learned, not where you've gone. If knowledge is power, where are the concentrations of power in your life history? What have you learned that sets you apart from others? Describe your resource of knowledge in an autobiographical paragraph:

For many people, where you've been and what you've done say more than anything else. What is your story? How are you set apart by life? What experience do you have that was worth the investment? Create another paragraph that tells your story from this perspective:

6. Your unique network

Twenty years ago, networks were nothing more than a group of broadcast stations under common control. Today, networks are flesh and blood. Rich people are still the ones who control networks, but these networks are alive.

Who do you know? Have you ever analyzed your network? How many people, really, do you know? Funeral directors have a good idea how to answer that question. Most mortuaries are designed around a funeral chapel that seats 250. This is not a chance determination; statistically, most people are in a network no larger than that. It is probable that no more than 250 souls will feel compelled to attend your funeral service.

If you are like most folks, you didn't recruit the people on your final guest list. Extended family members, people from work, neighbors who happened to buy the house across the street, the people who worked with you on committees—these are the faces who will greet your eulogizers. Unless, of course, you've done something about it first.

You can influence this list. You can decide whether you want that number to be larger or smaller, and you have ultimate control over who makes up that group, whatever size you choose.

The majority of us know only those people whom we have happened to meet on our way through life. We didn't try to remember them; they just kept running into us along the way and it was easier to archive their names for next time than it was to keep asking who they were. Social contact grew out of this consistent interaction. Friends became friends because of activity in common, nothing more. Most of us accept random selection for the most significant relationships of our lives.

There is a proactive minority, however. Watch out for them, they're really different! These are people who think and talk about the kinds of men and women they want to know, and then they go on safaris to find them. They think nothing of calling a perfect stranger (the more perfect the better) and introducing themselves brazenly: "Hi, you don't know me, but I would like to change that." They solicit the friends they want listed on their schedule of personal assets.

Whichever kind of person you are, you have a network. It may be your network by accident, or it may be your network by choice. The nature of your network affects your mission. Who you know can radically affect the course of your life.

At Christmas time, you scratch your head to list all the names, intimate and distant, that you want to spray with your greeting cards and xeroxed letters. In this next exercise, you'll need to think harder. We're not going for quantity here, but rather quality. The question is not, "How many people do you know?" but rather, "Who do you know that is most strategic?" List the ten people who are most integral to the quality of your life, both now and in the future. These are the ten individuals you definitely want to maintain access to in the future.

7. Your unique resources

A wise man once said that a person's life does not consist of the abundance of his possessions. He was right. That is not to say, however, that tangible resources have no impact on your life. The opposite is probably more accurate.

What you own says tons about you. The same sage said that your heart and your resources usually travel together. You put your money into the areas about which you are passionate. If you really believe in something, you will commit yourself to tangible expressions of it.

Two people with identical gifts, temperaments, experiences, and relationships can pursue substantially different missions in life because they are worlds apart in the area of resources. There is a serious and curious reason why that is true. There is evidence that the assets you hold and manage were placed in your hands intentionally, by God, and he plans for you to use them to advance his agenda, not yours.

That's a bold statement, but it needs to be said. I have often heard people state that a particular item is a blessing from God for something they did. That's a nice idea, but it doesn't hold water. God isn't yet passing out rewards; that comes later. Between now and then, God is investing his assets with his people to be used purposefully for him.

If above-average assets are under your control, you need to think seriously about some significant questions:

- Did God have a hand in your accumulating these resources?

- Has God had a part in your retaining those resources?

- Are there others you know who have worked as hard as you have, or harder, and not received what you have?

- If your possessions really belong to God and not to you, would he be happy with the way you are using them today?

- Does your financial plan reflect his ownership and his investment objectives, or does it reflect your own?

Even a cursory reading of the New Testament will demonstrate that the person with above-average financial resources has a decidedly greater responsibility before God than the less-endowed person.

One way to avoid the onus associated with this issue is to disavow existence of the problem: "What? I'm not rich!" Any English-speaking resident of a second-world country whose income is at or above the median for his area is rich according to global standards. So accept the mantle. Better to act rich and not be, than to be rich and fail the test of faithfulness.

Cheri and I managed a generous income for a number of years, and successfully controlled our lifestyle during that period. We had avoided consumer debt and were working toward retiring the mortgage on our family home. One of our greatest assets was the lack of debt, something unusual among people of our generation. Further, we had made it a practice to live on less than we made, and had worked to increase our financial support for causes we believed in. So our lives were fairly simple. This provided us with a fair amount of freedom because we didn't require all of the money I was capable of making. That was to significantly impact our life-purpose statement.

What are your unique resources? What do you have that most of the world doesn't? There are lots of folks in your acquaintance who don't know you well, but talk about you on the basis of what you have rather than what you are. In the space below, write down the things you possess that are most likely to be noted by these people:

8. Your unique allegiance

Bob Dylan flirted briefly with Christianity during the flexible middle years of his adult life. During that time, he released a number of songs with strong messages. One of them challenged listeners to accept this hard fact: You gotta serve somebody. There are no "free agents" in life. All of us are subservient to somebody. Dylan recognized only two options—we can serve the devil or we can serve the Lord.

Actually, one of those options has almost unlimited subsets. You may think you are extending your loyalty to some seemingly noble cause or ideology, but if it's anything other than the Lord, you have the wrong master.

Jesus said it this way:

No man can serve two masters. . . . He that isn't for me is against me.

Your life is either pointed toward the King of heaven and his agenda, or it is pointed somewhere else. Any direction other than toward God is a move away from him.

Why is this important? When you hammer out a personal statement of purpose, you have to know where it's headed. If you claim to offer your homage to Jesus Christ, your purpose must find itself within

his purpose for his Kingdom. If you are not allied
with God through personal submission, quite
frankly, any direction is equally viable. It doesn't
matter which way you're going, it's a short-term trip,
anyhow. But for the person tracking with God's purpose, this life is a warm-up for the main event!

Both Cheri and I are committed to the same
superior. We each entered into a life-changing relationship with Jesus Christ during our youth. We feel
no conflict over our individual expressions of submission to his lordship. In Palm Springs, this was an
easy conclusion: We were prepared to live out our
lives for his benefit. In the process, we would find
our own benefit.

The last great question of this list is the biggie:
Where is your unique allegiance? Only two choices
are possible—which team are you on?

Managing Your Life

We're now ready to look at the finished life-
purpose statement. Years ago, Cheri and I laid out
our discoveries about who we were and what we
had available to us. The result was the following
purpose statement:

> **Our life purpose** is to manage ourselves,
> our family, and our resources in a way that
> will allow us to cause biblical life-change

in business and professional men and women by teaching the timeless word of God, to the glory of God.

We have since discovered dozens of subsets and footnotes that spring from this simplified statement. But for more than ten years now, it has served to direct our decisions, and it looks like it will continue to take us through the remaining course of our adult lives.

Since our weekend in Palm Springs, Cheri and I have had many opportunities to teach friends and colleagues how to develop their own life-purpose statements. Here are some of their examples. Most are single-career or dual-career couples who are active in business as a profession:

> **Our life purpose** is to live a life that is so reflective of Christ dwelling in us that it will impact and communicate Christ's message of life-change to our family, our community, and as many other people as God directs to us, and to stretch to take hold of the future that God has for us, to the glory of God.

> **Our life purpose** is to enrich the lives of our family, friends, and those within our circle of influence by introducing and encouraging an approach to living centered around Jesus Christ, for the glory of God.

> **Our life purpose** is to be sensitive to those around us who are lost and that through seeking and building relationships we might influence decisions for Christ, while staying grounded in God's Word, in

the church, and in the fellowship of Christian friends, for the glory of God.

Our life purpose is to live a godly lifestyle, to know and understand God intimately, to bring as many people to faith in Christ as God allows, to equip and encourage Christians to do the same, and to generously support those who share this purpose, to the glory of God.

All of the eight areas we've covered represent distinguishing characteristics that make you different from everyone else. If you have thought these through and filled in the blanks, you have described a person (or, if you are married, a couple) who is set apart from every other individual on earth.

Your purpose, your mission in life, will be a natural pursuit for the wonderfully made, divinely designed individual you are. You are probably closer right now to answering the "Why am I here?" question than ever before.

Success for you is ultimately defined by your own sense of having pursued your unique purpose in life. The personal distinctives you have articulated in this section are the basis for drafting a life-purpose statement. Clarifying your purpose is a process that begins with the first draft and continues through the course of the rest of your life.

Your statement of life purpose should answer the question, "Why do I exist?" It is more specific than simply saying, "My life purpose is to glorify God." That is true for every person. It is true, but not unique. How do you glorify God? That is the question your statement should answer.

The night of his betrayal, Jesus prayed to his Father and expressed this truth: "I have brought you glory on earth by completing the work you gave me to do." That's the goal you should have for yourself as well—to complete the specific work God has given you to do on earth, and thus bring him glory.

As you write your life-purpose statement, here are two practical guidelines to keep in mind:

- Begin by listing all of the words, phrases and thoughts that seem to best describe the focus of your life.

- Continue simplifying your thoughts until they form one, nontechnical sentence which anyone can understand.

It's now time to write out your own purpose statement. Take whatever time is necessary to complete the following statement:

"My life purpose is to _____

_____

_____

_____

_____

for the glory of God."

CHAPTER SIX

Living on
Purpose

By this point, you've either taken the time to think through the elements of the purpose statement and have created a first-generation prototype for yourself, or you're waiting to see what else I've got to say before you take on any homework assignments.

Whichever approach you've selected, I hope you agree that the whole idea is intriguing. Interpersonal discussion seldom lands on the subject of life purpose. If we don't talk about it, it's doubtful we'll be driven to think about it, or more importantly, to do anything about it.

People who call a time-out to formalize their marching orders don't generally go around telling everyone they meet how they've chosen to live. You are more likely to find them about the business of living. The difference is that they've figured out which way they want to move . . . and they're moving. You may know some people who fit this profile. You've determined that something is subtly different about their manner, but you haven't put your finger on what it might be.

Let me give you some clues to help you recognize purpose-driven people:

- They're picky about the areas in which they choose to get involved. They aren't against what other people are doing, they just aren't over-committed to multiple projects. They have a rationale for deciding what they devote their time to.

- They appear to be more energized at the end of the day than at the beginning. Instead of dragging out to the parking lot after sundown, they seem undaunted from days that drain the rest of the team.

- They look like they enjoy their successes more than others. They don't display the lack of lasting satisfaction that often follows accomplishment. It almost seems that their achievements are leading to some bigger end, rather than ending up on a shelf, gathering dust.

- They have enough time for all the things they are trying to do. They aren't complaining about their schedules or load; when they need time off, they go, and they return refreshed and in control.

- They don't have hundreds of acquaintances, but they are known to have some really special friends. They don't talk to everybody, but when they're talking to you, they're really there—you feel like you're the only other person on the planet when you're with them.

- They talk about the future with a sense of anticipation and destiny—like they already know what it will be like, and it's exciting to consider arriving there to experience it.

- They portray no fear of the unknown—they don't seem to be flustered by things that upset those around them.

Purpose-driven people live with the benefits of a focused approach to life. They aren't like everyone else, but that doesn't bother them. They choose to be different in some of the most fundamental aspects of life.

This orientation to life is not without its difficulties. People who march to the tune of a different drummer stand out. People who stand out are not always commended. Accepting the potential of alienation is a necessary prerequisite, but it's worth that and more.

I want to encourage you to write out a personal mission statement if you haven't already. Even a bad one is better than none. If you have written one, it is valueless unless you evaluate what you do in light of that statement. This is the measuring stick by which you evaluate the things that require your energy, your time, and your resources.

How do you respond to the person who calls with a worthwhile activity that requires your time?

I've found tremendous satisfaction saying, "I'm excited about what you are doing. But it's not in line with my personal mission." It's interesting how quickly that caller hangs up; people don't know how to respond to a person who knows where he is going.

There are far too many people who die at age thirty, but aren't buried until seventy. What a tragedy to live out a meaningless four decades. Fortunately, that waste is not necessary.

If the idea of steering your life based on the dependable influence of a purpose statement is becoming attractive to you, you're ready to look at some of the ways such a life is expressed in the trenches. That's what the second half of this book is about.

We move now from the foundational and theoretical aspects of this discussion to the practical arena. This concept of purpose-driven living works when it causes conscious change in the way we live out each day. Here are the six areas we will explore:

- CONTROL: By retaining authority over your allocation of time, energy, and resources, you will progress toward your objectives rather than someone else's.

- FREEDOM: By rejecting the entanglement of possessive influences, you will be able to speak, move, and think in line with your life's purpose.

- COMMITMENT: By knowing the issues that are absolute, you will determine the essentials for allegiance to your cause; by protecting the values that define your life, you will illuminate your world.

- AVAILABILITY: By using an agenda rather than serving a schedule, you will have time for people who require compassionate attention even though they have no appointment.

- FOCUS: By narrowing your scope of target and objective, you will succeed in achieving deep and lasting impact.

- EXCELLENCE: By performing to your full potential, you will exceed the expectations of those who try to limit you to mediocrity.

For our model, I want to use the life of Jesus. You'll never meet a better example. This guy is amazing! In fact, the more you watch him in action, the more you wish you could be like him. You can.

We're going to concentrate on events that transpired during the last three years of Jesus' life. His public work provides case study after case study for our consideration and review.

If you could somehow learn to live like Jesus—the perfect, paramount expression of what God intended men and women to be—you'd never want to turn back. And you'd never recover. Neither would your world.

That's our agenda for part two.

CHAPTER SEVEN

Control

We're tempted to think that people who have "climbed the ladder" are in control of their lives. After all, how could they have made it that far without discipline? Too often, sadly enough, it just isn't so. Plenty of public examples demonstrate the point.

Senator Gary Hart was the front-runner for the 1988 Democratic presidential nomination. In one poll he led his nearest competitor by an incredible thirty-one points. He appeared to be a man with substance. Not content merely to throw slogans at the American people, he constantly studied and proposed challenging new ideas in the areas of national defense and economics.

Hart admitted he was a man with a mission. His mother had convinced him of his special calling in life. He attended divinity school, and though he later dropped any religious vocation, he continued to feel a firm call to serve the common good in high public office.

But something drastically malfunctioned on his way to the White House. Rumors about marital infidelity had circulated for years, and perhaps in an earlier era such indiscretions would have been ignored. But when photographers spied him on a private yacht with actress and model Donna Rice, and caught him again meeting Rice at his Washington, D.C. apartment, the resulting public furor forced him to bow out of the race.

Senator Hart seemed baffled that the public would examine the private areas of his character and judge them more important than his stated policies and intentions for the presidency. It seemed to him like a double standard—while the public expressed ever-increasing freedom in the sexual arena, it also demanded higher qualities of honor and trust in its public officials.

Gary Hart was a man on a mission. But that mission, in and of itself, couldn't prevent his downfall. One of his campaign advisors said, "His people assumed he *wanted* to be president and would discipline himself." They were right about what he wanted, but wrong in thinking that desire alone could generate the necessary discipline.

If we are to define total success in life, we must go beyond mission—as crucial as that is—and examine several essential qualities that allow a person to fulfill his mission. The first is *control*. By control, I mean consciously managing your allocation of time, energy, and resources. Only with such control can you progress toward your objectives.

But what does this control look like? We can cite many examples of individuals who are highly successful in one sphere but totally undisciplined in others. We admire professional athletes, at least in part, because they demonstrate incredible discipline to train and become the best in their sport. But this control on the playing field doesn't necessarily translate to success in marriage, business, or personal character. That's why we read about the tragedy of Pete Rose, major league baseball's all-time hit leader, who couldn't control an addiction to gambling. Or John Belushi, a spectacularly successful comedian and actor, who destroyed his life with drugs. Or Senator John Tower, who lost a chance to be Secretary of Defense because at one time he was unable to control his use of alcohol.

Examples of lack of control aren't always so spectacular. You might relate to the people who tell me they can't sustain relationships because of their travel schedule, and they feel they have no ability to influence it. Others depend on the use of caffeine and sleeping pills. I've sat in offices with men who keep a luxury car brochure in front of them. They believe life won't be meaningful unless they buy that machine . . . and it drives them to make more deals. Still others secretly crave those private moments when they can get another fix from pornographic magazines—hoping their spouse never discovers that addiction.

Fortunately, we have the perfect model of a man with a mission who also managed to control every area of his life. Public acclaim could not control him. After one remarkable day during which he healed many and gave powerful words of encouragement, he refused to heed the popular cry to spend more time with this adoring crowd. Why? He told his followers he had other villages to visit and other people to whom he had to preach. "That is why I have come," he said. He knew his purpose in life, and he didn't let popular opinion sway him from his course.

We know, of course, that this man was Jesus Christ—the most incredible example of control the world has ever seen. He provides a benchmark against which to measure ourselves. If you were to suggest the benchmark for a violin performer, you might name Itzhak Perlman. For a major league baseball pitcher, you might choose Orel Hershiser. But if you want a benchmark for a man with a mission who lived a controlled life, there is no one better than Jesus Christ. For thirty-three years, God lived on planet earth in the body of a man. This man faced the same demands, experienced the same drives, confronted the same external forces that we battle today, yet never allowed his life to get out of control.

Let's look at this remarkable life and see if we can learn any lessons about how to keep our lives under control.

Keep your appetites away from the wheel

One of the first things we learn about Jesus was how he handled temptation. After he was baptized by John the Baptist, Jesus took off for the wilderness.

After forty days of fasting and prayer, the tempter came and invited Jesus to use his power to turn stones into bread.

Now, there's nothing wrong with being hungry. Any of us who went forty hours without a meal would look for a place to load up. Jesus had every reason to be hungry after forty days without food. And even more significant, he had the power to do something about it—he could have changed the rocks into bread.

But he didn't do that. Instead, he said, "It is written that man does not live by bread alone, but on every word that comes from the mouth of God." Jesus was saying that he would be in control, not his appetites. While there's nothing wrong with eating, he wasn't going to let his hunger govern his resolve.

That's the temptation we all face. For the most part, our appetites are normal and legitimate. But problems develop when those appetites start to control our lives. Uncontrolled, those appetites can destroy us.

It's significant that Jesus resisted this temptation alone in the wilderness. That is where most of us have to win the battle. Today, more than ever, the control we exercise in private can significantly impact our life and mission.

Religious leaders struggle with this as much as anyone. Televangelist Jimmy Swaggart established his reputation by preaching against sin. He railed against immorality, pornography, and homosexuality. He exposed the indiscretions of Jim Bakker and another popular Pentecostal preacher. When asked about his own private life, he insisted it was under control. He told reporters that his wife, Frances, was with him wherever he went. "I'm never alone; I'm never by myself," he insisted.

No one knew that the sins he railed against were the very ones that held him in their grip. One of the pastors he exposed hired a private detective who produced photos proving Swaggart was seeing a prostitute. On television and news magazines, we saw a tearful Jimmy Swaggart begging forgiveness from his family, his congregation, and his God. He admitted he didn't have control of his appetites. Sadly, his appetites were at the wheel controlling him.

Schedule sufficient time for rest and relaxation

Many people in the work place no longer punch a time clock. They choose when to start and when to stop. Their work day is defined by projects and accomplishments rather than by hours. This is especially true for those who have attained the great American dream of working for themselves.

A few years ago I conducted an informal survey among small business owners. One of the areas of inquiry concerned vacation habits. Most of these men and women had left positions with other firms to go off on their own. At their previous employment, they had enjoyed an average of three weeks of vacation each year. They told me that one of the motivations for starting their own business was the chance to free up more leisure time. When you're the boss, they told themselves, you can be gone more. You aren't hindered by personnel policies that limit your freedom.

My findings were humorous but sad. On the average, these independent entrepreneurs had been on their own for about five years. During that time, none had ever taken more than two weeks of vacation in any given year. And none of them had been gone for more than one week at a stretch in the previous year. Despite their original intent, they didn't believe they could be gone any more than that. The very move that was supposed to increase their opportunities for rest instead increased the need while reducing the supply.

Jesus faced that same tension. He was inundated by crowds. From dawn to dusk he faced demands from people. It was enough to make anyone tired. Jesus recognized that and did something about it—both for himself and his associates.

One time, Jesus sent the twelve disciples on a preaching journey. When they returned, Jesus saw they were both enthusiastic and exhausted, but crowds still pressed on him so much that there wasn't even time to eat. So Jesus said, "Let's go away to a quiet place and get some rest."

To translate into today's vernacular, Jesus was saying, "Guys, the fact that the phones are ringing constantly and the schedule is jammed full is no reason to say we can't get away. If we need to rest, then we're going to go and rest."

Jesus did this throughout his ministry. He frequently escaped from the crowds and found a quiet place in the wilderness to pray. This quiet time was essential. It was the way he kept perspective, kept control over his schedule, and recognized his priorities.

Some people find this time early in the morning or late at night. They take a few minutes every day to pray, read the Bible, and meditate. We need this kind of time daily. In addition, we need longer stretches away from the hustle and pressures of our careers.

Maintain the right to select your associates

One of the important news stories after a president is elected is the naming of his cabinet and other key posts. The day after President Bush was elected as the forty-first President of the United States, it was announced that James Baker would be his Secretary of State. Next, Bush invited Nicholas Brady to remain on as Treasury Secretary. He bypassed recommendations from his advisors and named John Sununu, governor of New Hampshire, as his Chief of Staff. And so it went. Almost every day there were new announcements of major appointments.

Perhaps even more important than his highly visible appointments were the secondary level choices—the sub-cabinet-level officials, the under-secretaries—who would have primary roles in forming and executing policies of the new president. Without these key players, the president would have little hope of achieving his agenda.

Choosing the right associates is as critical for us as it is for a new president. We see this very clearly in the life of Jesus. One day, Jesus rode a boat across the Galilee Lake to a country called Gergesa. There he met a wild man who lived in caves and was so strong that he could break the chains locals used to contain him. Jesus confronted this man and ordered the demons to depart. It must have been an incredible sight, for the people of the region were so afraid they begged Jesus to leave.

As Jesus boarded his boat, the man who had been demon-possessed begged to go with him. I can sympathize with this man's request—he wanted to spend time with this remarkable person who had just freed him. But Jesus wouldn't hear of it. "Go home to your family and tell them how much the Lord has done for you, and how he has had mercy on you," Jesus said.

Why did Jesus refuse this man's request? Would it have made that much difference, adding one more person to his team—especially someone so obviously grateful? The answer is found in the way he chose his associates. Earlier in his career, as Jesus gained popularity, he found himself surrounded by more and more disciples. It was becoming unmanageable. Further, Jesus recognized that if he was going to accomplish his mission, he needed to spend quality time with a handful of men. He simply could not effectively train such a large group.

So one night, Jesus went off alone to a mountain and spent the entire night in prayer. The next morning, he called all of his followers together and chose twelve to be his disciples. For the remaining years of his ministry, while he didn't ignore the multitudes, he concentrated on these twelve men. The point is clear—Jesus, after careful thought and prayer, chose the men he wanted around him. They didn't choose him.

Some of you are surrounded by people who have taken control of your life. They call you and dictate where you'll be tonight, what you'll do this weekend, what projects you will do next, and how you will spend your casual hours. They have decided to influence, perhaps even direct, your life.

If the people who occupy your life are people you did not choose to fill that role, your life is out of control. You're living under the direction of others. Jesus modeled a far different approach. He chose where his time would be spent. If someone had called him on the phone and said, "We've got to get together right now," he might well have said, "Not necessarily." Do you realize that you don't have to accept every invitation and appointment?

"Oh, great," you might be thinking, "this is my chance to get out of this marriage. I just wasn't thinking when I got into this relationship, and now I'm going to take control."

Sorry, but no way. If you're involved in relationships with people by covenant (as in marriage), or by contract (as in a business situation), then you stick to your guns in that relationship for the term of the agreement (for marriage, that's for life!).

I'm talking about those situations where you have accepted a responsibility that really isn't there. Let me give you an example.

I was talking recently with a business executive who was losing interest in her husband. There wasn't any glaring inadequacy, she just found herself examining him critically in private and becoming irritated over petty things. I asked what she thought might be driving her new attitude toward him.

Turns out, she had been lunching almost daily with some other professional women for some time, and all three of the others had been divorced in the last five years. None of them had any good thing to say about their "ex." She found herself unengaged in the conversations but quietly internalizing what she was hearing over lunch.

She concluded that the benefits to be gained from her time with her friends were less important than the damage it was doing to her marriage. Any obligation she had to them was self-imposed. She needed to get control before her internal struggles became openly damaging to her marriage.

It's easy to find yourself in those kinds of relationships. Perhaps there are people with whom you spend time who have the potential to keep you from being everything you could otherwise be. Are you avoiding taking control of those types of friendships? Don't avoid it!

Reject any advancement that will assure your decline

Not long ago, I was with a man who lost a close race for Congress. Since he lost by only a few votes, there was plenty of potential for remorse over what might have been. He, however, was not at all dejected; he was becoming increasingly glad for the loss. "Great solons aren't necessarily great fathers," he told me. He saw that political victory might have brought personal defeat. For him, the emotional, adrenaline-driving work of Congress wasn't compatible with being an effective father.

It's a good thing this man didn't have to learn the lesson the hard way. This is one of the hardest things to realize—to see our limitations and decide not to exceed them. Recently, I met with a friend who's in senior management for a billion-dollar company. He was lamenting the personal cost of his high-level position. He is seriously considering going to the CEO with a request to move one rung *down* the corporate ladder. Why? He finds himself envious of friends whose lesser positions grant them a higher quality of life. He said he's been had by the allure of the boardroom, and now he wants out.

How do we know whether to accept, or even pursue, a higher position? The answer goes back to mission. Unless we know our purpose in life, we don't know our limits. Even when we know our mission, the temptation inevitably comes to exceed it. Control means knowing whether that advancement fits with our mission, and acting accordingly.

Jesus faced this temptation. He had just preached to a huge crowd—perhaps as many as twenty thousand people (five thousand men, plus women and children). Now the people were hungry, and Jesus performed one of his most memorable miracles. With a boy's lunch of five loaves and two small fish, he fed the entire assembly. Not only that, the disciples gathered twelve baskets full of leftovers.

The people were impressed. They quickly saw all kinds of possibilities. Jesus would make the perfect king! He would overthrow the Roman occupiers! With Jesus as king, they would never go hungry! They also suspected, however, that Jesus wouldn't accept a formal request, so they laid plans to force him to be their ruler. But Jesus knew what was happening; he dismissed the crowd and immediately withdrew to a mountain to be alone.

My friend Bill received a call from "The Man" in a Fortune 500 company. It was the last person he expected to hear from. What was more, the call was to offer him a position he'd worked for all of his professional life: "We want you to take over our Minneapolis office." Implied in that invitation was the chance for corporate management on the highest level a few years down the road.

Isn't it obvious what Bill should do? As some might say, it's a no-brainer. Why even pray about it? Isn't God's will obvious here?

But Bill did pray about it. While this was the position he'd hoped for, the job meant moving his family two thousand miles. He and his wife were just starting to see significant results from their investment in the lives of men and women they'd befriended over the years. The advancement would uproot them from that field. It would take years to reestablish the kind of relationships they now enjoyed. The more he prayed and thought about the opportunity, the more he realized it wasn't right for him.

I know many people with Fortune 500 companies who have lived in places they never even knew existed. Most of them would never go back to these places, but they were necessary stops toward their ultimate objective. When the company said "Jump," they answered, "How high?" They knew they might be forgiven once for refusing a move, but not twice. And yet for many of them, the advancement was not in their best interests.

That's the scenario here with Jesus. He recognized that a promotion to king was the worst thing he could do. In essence, he said, "You can keep this honor. That's not why I have come."

Managing Your Life

While nothing is more convicting than examining the recent history of our own lives, there is no better way to stay on track with our mission. I suggest you take out your personal schedule for the last two weeks and review it in light of what has been said about "control." Go through each line item in your datebook and put a number by each item where you have violated one of the four principles of control we've examined:

#1—Appetite-driven decision

#2—Needed rest but kept on going

#3—Gave time to someone I could not afford

#4—Enticed by position that isn't for me

Once you've reviewed your datebook, go back and count the times each number is noted. The number with the highest score deserves prompt attention.

CHAPTER EIGHT

Freedom

Mention the word *freedom* and many of us conjure up images of the sexual revolution, "I've got to be me," punk hair cuts, and alternative lifestyles.

But that is not what freedom means for those involved in total life management. For men and women with mission, freedom is rejecting the entanglement of possessive influences so they are able to speak, move, and think in line with their life's purpose.

Contemporary society fosters a subtle form of slavery. Though we believe we overcame that problem a century ago, it continues today in ways we seldom seriously consider. The degree of impairment may vary, but the lack of freedom is rampant.

Just how free are you today? If you were to travel anywhere in the world and ask average people, "What is the most free place in the world to live?" most would answer, "America." Based on what they read and see on television, they are convinced that the United States is the land of ultimate freedom. You can wear what you want, eat anything you like, do whatever you please. There are no limits.

Of course, that picture is illusory. We only have to look at the statistics of people addicted to some mind-altering drug or lifestyle to know how untrue it is. But there is a more subtle form of bondage that many don't recognize.

The only thing more pitiful than a person who is a slave and knows it is a person who's a slave yet thinks he is free. We in the United States live among a society of slaves.

I visited a man in his high-rise office in Los Angeles. From his desk he enjoyed a marvelous view of the city. The man worked for one of those companies where your elevator stop reflects the amount of power you have. Those who exit before you are underlings. The ones who stay on after you get off are called "Sir" or "Ma'am." This man's place in the pecking order was rising dramatically.

As we looked out the window into a beautiful plaza, I noticed some people sitting on the benches, in no hurry to go anywhere. I asked my friend, "How free do you feel?"

"Are you kidding?" he responded. "I've never before had the freedom I have now."

"Let me rephrase that." I pointed to the plaza, noting that some of the people there probably didn't have a home beyond the bench where they would lay their heads that night. "I would propose that some of those people down there are more free than you are."

My friend didn't believe me.

"You know, the weather in Florida is incredible right now," I said. "Why don't you come with me and we'll spend a couple of weeks on the beach in Miami?"

"Now you're just making a hypothetical proposition," he protested.

"Let's pretend I'm serious. Do you want to go with me?"

"I'd love to, but I can't."

"Why not?"

He opened up his desk calendar and showed me. His appointment schedule looked like the final days of a presidential campaign.

"How much notice would you need to be able to get away for two weeks?" I asked.

"Bob, I haven't had a two-week vacation in years," came the sad reply.

"Look down below. In that plaza right now, if I showed up with some prepaid tickets, I could get a bus load of people to go with me to Miami. They're free to go now, and you're not. So who's more free?"

About this time, our allowed time was up. I'm afraid he felt better before I came than when I left. But the point was clear. My friend wasn't really free.

The point of this discussion was not to say that freedom allows us to do anything we want when we want. Rather, the question is: Are you able to call the shots in your life, or are you living with chains wrapped around your leg?

The most free person who ever walked planet earth was Jesus. In fact, he said he came "to proclaim freedom for the prisoners." To my knowledge, there is no record of Jesus ever visiting a prison. Certainly the freedom he proclaimed was for literal prisoners, but I believe he also made this statement for people who were prisoners of daily life—prisoners of the things that controlled them.

How was Jesus free? We can look at how he didn't worry about where he would sleep, or what he would eat and drink. That's nothing, you say—you don't worry about that either. But Jesus didn't have a home to call his own, and often didn't know where his next meal was coming from. Howver, he never considered it a burden; rather, he was free to come and go as his mission demanded. There were no mortgage payments, no utility bills, no worrying about grocery shopping and meal planning.

Am I suggesting, then, that we follow this pattern? Should we walk away from our homes and forget about stopping at the grocery store? No. Rather, these things don't occupy our mind. We are free to concentrate on fulfilling our purpose in life. The person in bondage worries about how he will pay his bills. All of his credit cards are at the limit. He dreads the arrival of the mailman, who might bring another notice of overdue payment. He's constantly worried about getting out of debt, and his only hope is that Ed McMahon will call his number. Certainly we would agree this person is not free.

Jesus demonstrated freedom for us in a number of ways. Let's look at four of them.

Keep yourself free from ineffective traditions

Zig Ziglar tells about a family preparing to celebrate Christmas. John was home from the office and hanging around the kitchen. His wife, Mary, was scurrying around him as she prepared the ham for the oven. As part of her ritual, she cut off the end of the ham and set it aside. "Why did you do that?" John asked.

"That's the way my mom always did it," was her quick response.

Fortunately, Mary's mother was in the living room, so John continued to pursue an explanation for the hacked-off ham. "Mom, why do you cut off the end of the ham?" he asked.

"I don't know," she answered. "I learned it from my mother."

Now John was really curious. He decided to call up Grandma in Indiana. After exchanging the necessary pleasantries, he asked, "Grandma, why did you always cut off the end of your ham before you baked it?"

There was a moment of silence before Grandma answered: "Because my pan was too short."

It doesn't take long before a reasonable response to a practical situation becomes a tradition. By the time a second generation enters the picture, armies can form to protect the sanctity of a practice that originally had little importance.

One day Jesus had a run-in with some masters of tradition. They were called Pharisees and they taught the law to the Jewish people. These teachers asked Jesus, "Why don't your disciples live according to the tradition of the elders instead of eating their food with 'unclean' hands?"

Now, these men weren't talking about washing their dirty hands before dinner. They demanded people perform a ceremonial cleaning anytime before they ate. Why? Because the elders, the folks who lived in previous generations, had established the tradition.

If you ever wanted to find a society where tradition was king, you couldn't do much better than first-century Israel. Jesus grew up in this culture, but how did he respond when challenged? He called the Pharisees "hypocrites" because they enforced human traditions while ignoring the commands of God. He didn't deny all tradition, but insisted that tradition without substance has no value.

Many people suffer from the same problem in America; Lifestyle and values have been shaped by corporate public relations departments. Perhaps you remember when you graduated from business school and entered the work force. At first, you offered bold and fresh approaches to problems, thinking this was the way to move up the ladder. After all, if you found a way to do things better, everyone would rise up and call you blessed . . . right?

Well, they do rise up, but it's not blessed they call you. Perhaps you've pulled a few arrows out of your posterior. You've been bruised by floating an idea that no one wanted to hear, even though you're convinced it's an improvement over the way it's always been done.

After you've heard the words "we've always done it this way" and you've had your nose broken a few times trying to change things, you finally give up. You decide you'll live within the confines of the traditional approach.

Jesus said he wasn't bound to ineffective tradition. He said he would do anything necessary to be effective. Tradition did not govern his methods, his mission did.

Don't be hindered by unhealthy relationships

Jesus was beginning to have tremendous public appeal. Crowds flocked to him to hear him speak and receive his healing touch. And how did his family feel about this? Not as you might expect. In fact, open hostility soon broke out between Jesus and his brothers.

The four half-siblings of Jesus—James, Joseph, Simon, and Judas—really got exercised over their elder brother and his widespread acclaim. Knowing that a plot was rumored to be brewing among the Jewish leadership to dispose of Jesus, they came to him just days before a major religious festival took place in Jerusalem.

Their advice? "You ought to go up to Jerusalem and show the crowds what you can do! If you're really who you say you are, that's where you belong. If you are overselling yourself and really can't deliver, then stay away." Their cynicism was thinly veiled; Jesus knew exactly what they meant. His public image wasn't on their minds. Their lives would have been simpler, in their view, with him out of the picture.

Jesus sent them up to Jerusalem without him, and later quietly went there alone. It was better for him to spend the holiday alone than with these men who chose to distance themselves from him and his purposes.

For some people, the most traumatic time of the year is the holiday season. I've talked to people who would rather scratch November and December off their calendar than go through the obligatory family gatherings. The reason is that their family is committed to their demise.

Too many people are chained to unhealthy relationships. They feel obligated to listen to and be swayed by people who want to destroy them. Jesus honored his family, but that didn't mean he had to agree with them.

An executive recently described to me his experience as the majority partner in a family business. During a particularly stressful time in the company's business cycle, he began to feel distance between himself and his father and brothers. He could not understand it, but the demands of declining revenues and operating losses kept him distracted from relational issues.

One afternoon, his accountant called him at the office. My friend was aghast as he heard how his father and brothers had hired an investigator and an attorney to examine his activities. They had contacted the firm's CPA to obtain financial information in an effort to construct a case of malfeasance against their son and brother.

With nothing to hide, the CEO encouraged his accountant to cooperate with the effort, knowing there was no risk to him. After waiting a few weeks to let his emotions cool, he confronted his family members with what he had heard.

They admitted they were looking for evidence of surreptitious dealings that could explain the company's current woes. They simply did not believe his explanation of the facts. Grudgingly, they admitted they had been unable to discover even one element of dishonesty in his conduct. Even then they still said they didn't trust him.

The *coup de grâce* came when the invoices arrived for the services of the investigator and attorney. The innocent CEO was asked to foot the bill for his own inquisition!

It's a fact that we don't choose our family. Some of our friendships and associates come without our choice, too. When those relationships impact us negatively, we need to adjust. Not that we ignore them, but we don't have to let them govern our lives. The people I need to be with most are those who believe what I believe, not the people who shared an address with me before I had a choice in the matter.

Avoid the stress of unrealistic expectations

I was driving home after dark and came to a stop at a traffic light. Across the street stood a familiar office building, and on the top floor, on the northeast corner, the lights still blazed. It happened that the tenth floor housed a friend of mine named Sean.

From my car phone, I dialed Sean on his private line. He answered and I asked, "What are you doing there at this hour?"

"I can't leave yet. I'm not finished," he replied weakly.

Now, I'd known Sean for more than a decade. He's a "Type A" poster kid. Evenings, weekends, Sunday mornings, he's liable to be caught with his briefcase open. In all the years I've known him, he's never gotten finished yet.

"Hey, listen friend," I said. "If you stay there all night, will you be able to finish what you're working on?"

The pause cost me thirty-five cents on the car phone. Finally, he admitted, "No."

"Well, since you can't finish anyway, I'm giving you permission to go home. I'll call your wife to tell her to expect you. I'm not moving from this corner until I see your lights go out." Sure enough, within a minute the lights were out and Sean was released from his self-imposed slavery to an unreasonable expectation.

Sean isn't terribly peculiar. Most men and women I know who have made it to responsible career positions believe they should do twice what their priorities say they should. They act as if God had inspired the writing of their job descriptions, and they're willing to die trying to live up to the responsibilities described in that document.

Maybe it's time to reexamine your personal expectations of performance, or those imposed on you by your superiors. Some people succumb to marching orders that should never have been given, and they never take the time to contest them.

If one thing impresses me about Jesus, it's that he was definitely not stressed by unrealistic expectations. Have you noticed that Jesus carried no Daytimer? We see him going from town to town, from village to village, teaching in the synagogues, preaching to the crowds, healing the sick. We're told that when he saw the crowds, he had compassion on them. He stopped, spent time with them, and met them at their place of need.

But he couldn't do it all. In the midst of a particularly demanding day, he told his disciples that the harvest was plentiful but the workers were few. They should pray for God to send more workers. In other words, Jesus needed help!

When we learn about God, we discover that he transcends time. One day for him is like a thousand years, and a thousand years is like a day. Now, I've spent some days at the office that seemed like a thousand years. But this is different. God stepped into time and spent thirty-three-and-a-half years facing the same time constraints that we face. Jesus had three-and-a-half years to fulfill his mission. There was more to do than one person could do. What would our culture tell him? Work nights. Work Saturday and Sunday. Cancel your vacation. But never admit that there's more than you can handle. That's un-American!

Has anyone come to you and suggested that you go home when the sun goes down, or that you take a vacation? If so, you're fortunate. Most companies I know are willing to allow you to operate on the most unrealistic expectations. Jesus wasn't like that. He knew what he could do. When he reached his limit, he said, "Hey, why don't you guys call headquarters and ask for reinforcements? There's more than we can do here."

If Jesus had limited capacity as a human being, doesn't that suggest that we're limited, too? If he couldn't do it all, it's unlikely that you and I can do it all. But I know many people who live with a chain of unrealistic expectations firmly locked around their legs. They're in slavery. They say they can't leave because there's more to do. Perhaps they don't need more time, they need more help.

If you're feeling bound to the office, if you feel you can't ever get it all done, you have permission to admit your limits. It's okay to shut off the lights, to go home and spend time with your family. Take a break!

See through the attraction of temporary prosperity

Cheri and I had decided to spend a quiet New Year's Eve with our friends John and Kay. After a great dinner, we spread out the Monopoly game to pass the time before midnight. With hours to play out the game to a win-lose conclusion, I quickly got into the spirit. This was Wall Street on the dining room table.

Our personality differences soon became apparent in the strategies we employed. John acquired a few properties that he developed extensively while I employed a more diversified strategy—utilities, transportation, and a wide spread of residential real estate. Kay was challenging my lead as we competed for control, while Cheri spent her money like a sailor on leave—blissfully enjoying the trip around the board.

As my wife ran low on funds, she happened upon the hotel-ridden Boardwalk controlled by John "Trump." "I can't pay the rent," she sighed as John read the numbers from the back of the card.

John smiled and said, "That's okay! Pay me when you can."

Kay and I exploded. "If she can't come up with the dough, she's outta here!" I railed. "That's the point of the game—there's winners and losers. And she's a loser!"

As soon as the words were out of my mouth, I

could see it was going to be a long drive home. I had committed a cardinal mistake—I forgot we were playing a game. I was so caught up in making deals that it became reality in my mind. I risked marital harmony for the holiday weekend just to load up my stack of play money.

Life's not really that different. Business is just a big Monopoly game, yet most of us treat it like it's the main event. The more I understand what Jesus taught, the more aware I am that one of these days God is going to come along, tap us on the shoulder and say, "The game's over." Then he's going to pick up the board, slide all of the pieces back into the box, and call it quits.

Jesus talked a lot about money. Have you ever thought about what money is for? Jesus says this is what it is for: "Use worldly wealth to gain friends for yourselves, so that when it is gone you will be welcomed into eternal dwellings."

"Now wait a minute!" you protest. "God is saying to use money to buy friends? I thought you were supposed to use money to buy stocks or cars or houses or income-producing property." No, Jesus said to use money to buy friends. Why? He says you can either use temporary money to buy temporary things, or you can use temporary money to buy eternal things. Is it better merely to trade on the Monopoly board, or to take Monopoly money and buy something of real value? Smart people use money in a way that will benefit them for a long period, not just a short time.

A trader in Chicago employs this perspective of Jesus. His name is Mark Ritchie, and he is a co-founder of a highly successful commodities trading group, which by 1988 was the largest options trading group in the world. Ritchie's success in business has translated into financial abundance.

While his contemporaries pursue excesses, Ritchie pursues a mission. Six years ago, he formed his own international development agency with a desire to help poor people become independent through his group's assistance. He uses his wealth to help people in need, thus producing lasting impact. His passion? "I would like to take a poor guy and give him an opportunity to create wealth."

That's "using worldly wealth to gain friends for yourselves, so that when it is gone you will be welcomed into eternal dwellings."

The Pharisees were the televangelists of their day. They heard Jesus say this and sneered at him. He had an answer for them, too. "You are the ones who justify yourselves in the eyes of men," he said. "God knows your hearts. What is highly valued among men is detestable in God's sight."

Now, that's a sobering thought: What is highly valued among men is detestable to God. He was specifically talking to people who love money. God says they had the wrong value system. His value system says use temporary things (like money) for eternal purposes.

Jesus spent no time trying to accumulate temporary wealth. Do you know why? Simply put—why spend time chasing something that's temporary when you can spend the same time chasing the eternal? That makes sense to me. The problem is that I don't think about it often enough.

Managing Your Life

1) Review the following and rate yourself from one to ten—with ten being totally free and one meaning you are totally in bondage:

    a) Bound to ineffective traditions

    b) Distracted by unhealthy relationships

    c) Stressed by unrealistic expectations

    d) Enamored by temporary prosperity

2) Pick the one with the lowest score. What is one thing you can do in this area to move towards greater freedom?

3) Commit yourself to implement your plan in this area within the next week.

CHAPTER NINE

Commitment

A homebuilding company in my community enjoys a reputation for integrity and quality. While the principals in the company are Christian, they attract respect rather than scorn because of their philosophy and conduct. Their unusual status is due, in part, to an exercise they undertook when the company was founded.

Before they tackled their first commercial venture, the company founders huddled together to define their corporate values. What emerged were the "Fieldstone Values"—six statements of ethical foundation that have been the keystone of operations ever since. Every employee at the Fieldstone

Company is instructed in these values. On every desk is a business-card-sized summary of these values. Every employee also carries them in a pocket. At each Christmas party, awards are given to the employees who have demonstrated exemplary performance within each of the six values.

Fieldstone takes these essentials seriously. Workers are not disciplined for mistakes that cost the firm money. Rather, they are disciplined for decisions at odds with the company's values, even if the decision profited the corporation. To them, values are more important than income.

One of the partners in the company told me about a decision made by a middle manager that ended up costing the firm over $150,000. In most other companies, the manager would have been fired. It was the type of situation where a corporation's values are shown to be real or mere window dressing.

The scenario was reviewed in light of the company values, and it was determined that the manager made his moves in keeping with them. Though he cost the firm money through the option he had chosen, the only other choice available would have violated those values. Because he made a value-based decision, he was commended, though it cost Fieldstone handsomely. Now there's a firm more interested in protecting its credibility than its capital.

As I write this, the latest Wall Street scandal is playing out in the bankruptcy proceedings of Drexel Burnham Lambert, Inc. During the mid-1980s, Drexel was the hottest, most profitable firm on Wall Street. Under the leadership of Michael Milken, it fueled some of the biggest and nastiest hostile corporate takeovers in history. The terms associated with Milken and Drexel—high-yield junk bonds, insider trading, leveraged buyouts, arbitrage—came to symbolize the greed of big-time corporate raiders. Reportedly they cared little that their push for huge personal profits might cost the jobs of individual employees as assets were sold to pay off immense debt.

It would be interesting to see a daily truth index included with the Dow Jones Industrial Average and other stock exchange quotes. For many, truth is no longer objective and absolute. It has become a drifting value that moves up or down based on the morals of the day. An increasing percentage of the population views truth as vacillating, unreal, and nebulous. The standard is public image, not getting caught, and making as much money as possible.

But there are some, like Fieldstone, who hold that values are important—more important than short-term profit, for they define who you are and your reputation. These people aren't necessarily unsuccessful. On the contrary, their success can often be attributed to their values. It's this commitment that defines life and gives it meaning.

Of what does this commitment consist? I submit there are two essential elements—a set of basic core values, and a willingness to defend those values when they are attacked.

Clarify the core values worth defending

It is popular to denounce people as dogmatic when they hold strong views. By knowing the issues that are absolute, however, we can determine when and how to defend our cause. Separating nonessential opinion from inviolate truth is the first step. If there are inarguable realities, dogmatism is called for and appropriate.

Henry Ward Beecher once said, "Whatever is only almost true is quite false, and among the most dangerous of errors because being so near truth, it is most likely to lead astray." Many people like to play horseshoes with the truth, saying that close is good enough. Dogmatic people are viewed with alarm, for they threaten the security of others.

Many people feel safe when they are free to redefine truth subjectively. When someone gets loose in the camp preaching the idea of moral absolutes, the person with a "whatever turns you on" credo gets unsettled. Dogmatic people can really be irritating with their message of invariable standards of right and wrong!

There are three classes of issues. The first level concerns things that are irrelevant. It doesn't matter that we disagree at this level. We may compare the color of our cars. You may say red is the best, and I will say blue. Now, while I may say your car is nice, I'll be thinking, *I'd never buy a car that color.* But it won't have anything to do with our relationship.

At level two are issues on which compromise is possible. If we're in business together and deciding about building a fleet of cars, I might prefer Chrysler and you might want to go with General Motors. The decision isn't crucial to the direction of the company, so we decide to compromise—we buy Mercedes instead. There should be many areas where we are willing to give ground because foundational issues are not at stake.

It's at level three where we find the nonnegotiables. These are those few issues about which we must be dogmatic. This is bedrock truth, to be defended at all costs.

Jesus was a perfect example of someone who had clearly defined his core values. As we examine his life, we see there were many areas where he was willing to compromise. In fact, that was one reason he got into so much trouble with religious authorities, for he did not consider their traditions inviolable. Just what were his core values? We may be surprised at the things he considered absolute:

The purity of religion

Shortly after Jesus began his public ministry, he visited Jerusalem. Passover, the most important Jewish festival, was about to begin. In the outer courtyard of the temple Jesus found a rowdy marketplace. Large amounts of money were being exchanged and sacrificial cattle, sheep, and doves were being sold at inflated rates. It was a lot like the way Christmas has become commercialized in our own time, burying the significance of the birth of the Christ child.

How did Jesus respond? He made a whip and drove the merchandizers out of the temple, along with their animals. "Get these out of here!" he shouted. "How dare you turn my Father's house into a market!"

Today, we find many people turned off by Christianity because of the corruption of some of its highly visible media preachers. These televangelists have used religion as a marketable item from which to draw a tremendous financial return. They've corrupted the purity that God intended.

Perhaps one reason Jesus got so upset with the market inside the temple was that it stood in the Court of the Gentiles, where non-Jews were permitted. It was intended as a place where people from all over the world could come to find out about God. But instead of encountering God, they were separated from their money. Jesus considered that a defamation of God's character. (We'll look later at the way Jesus confronted this problem.)

The necessity of conversion

Shortly after the temple confrontation, a man named Nicodemus came to see Jesus. Nicodemus was a highly regarded religious leader. If you lived in Israel and had any questions about religion, Nicodemus was the man to see. Religiously speaking, he was top dog.

But even Nicodemus recognized that Jesus had a supernatural authority. Jesus shocked him by saying, "No one can see the kingdom of God unless he is born again." He meant that unless we are supernaturally transformed, we'll never be a part of God's plan. There must be a moment of conversion.

Perhaps you are like many people today who consider themselves Christians. They assume affiliation with God because of their connection to a recognized church or because they've been raised in a home by parents who held Christian beliefs. When asked about religion, most North Americans probably aren't going to say they're Moslem or Buddhist. So of course, they're Christian.

Jesus disputed all that. He said we are not Christian because of upbringing or affiliation. If we are Christians, it is because we have made a conscious decision to surrender to the Spirit of God. Jesus was dogmatic about that. Unless you buy into this bedrock truth, you are separated from him.

The exclusivity of Christianity

Jesus made some audacious statements in his life. For instance, he said, "I am the way and the truth and the life. No one comes to [God] the Father except through me." Jesus didn't say he was "a" way or "a" truth or "a" life. He used the definite article. He was not one option among many, but the only way to reach God.

If you're involved in distribution, you know how valuable a territory is when you own exclusive rights to it. How valuable would those rights be if, after you've paid a hefty fee to represent that product or service, you discover that many others have the same right to provide the same product to the same customers? An exclusive right means that in your market area no other source exists to obtain your product. People have to come directly to you or they can't obtain the product.

Jesus said he had an exclusive right to represent God on planet earth. Try to call God the Father direct, and he will direct all calls back to Jesus. There are a lot of people trying to figure out a way to make room for anyone who worships the great cosmos in the sky—as long as that person is sincere. "You don't need Jesus, you don't need the Cross; there are other ways to heaven." Not according to Jesus! He says he's the only authorized distributor, and if you don't go through him, you don't get the product. It's that simple.

You want to be called dogmatic? Tell people that Christianity provides the only way to get to heaven. They'll say you are dogmatic, and they'll be right. But if Jesus spoke the truth, we can't afford not to make this a core value.

The window of opportunity

Finally, Jesus was intensely dogmatic about our window of opportunity. He said, "You are from below; I am from above. You are of this world; I am not of this world. I told you that you would die in your sins; if you do not believe that I am the one I claim to be, you will indeed die in your sins."

That's pretty narrow, isn't it? A lot of people believe in the second chance. They somehow think that after they die, God will take them to a little waiting room and say, "This is your last chance, buddy." That's not what Jesus said. He spoke of a window of opportunity, and if you miss it, it's gone forever.

We're all familiar with this concept in day-to-day life. If you want to take advantage of certain tax breaks, you have to act before December 31. If you want to respond to a business proposition or take advantage of a market share, you have to act according to a time frame—the opportunity won't last forever. If you want to buy your spouse a Christmas or Valentine's gift, you have to act before December 25 or February 14.

Concerning the biggest deal we will ever face in life, Jesus said there is a window of opportunity. The one difference between this one and the others is that for the IRS or a holiday gift, there is a countdown—we know exactly when it will happen. But we don't know when life will end. It could be fifty years from now. It could be tomorrow.

Jesus was dogmatic about this. He called this truth. Some people will find themselves eternally in a place they never planned to be because they didn't understand that one day the window would close—their chance would pass. Their opportunity to say yes to Jesus and to what he wanted to be in their lives would be gone forever.

The apostle Paul claimed the gospel was so simple that the intelligent would tend to dismiss it as foolish. "Trust Jesus Christ and what he did for us two thousand years ago, surrender our lives to him, and believe that this will change our eternal destiny? That's too easy!" That's right, it is. But that's the gospel. It's our choice to do something about it.

Now, it's not enough merely to hold some fundamental convictions. Total life management requires that we defend those values when they are under attack. Jesus, the perfect man, also showed us how to do that.

Defend basic core values when they are attacked

If a vote were taken pitting harmony against conflict, harmony would win hands down. It is for that reason that confrontation is often devalued. When harmony is held in highest esteem, however, the potential for serious error multiplies. If we value truth, then confrontation must occur.

Jesus wasn't afraid of confrontation. Some of the most dramatic scenes in the Bible are those where Jesus debated the religious and political leaders of his day. When religious leaders questioned why he ate with "undesirables" like tax collectors, he could have ignored them. But he confronted them saying, "It is not the healthy who need a doctor, but the sick. I have not come to call the righteous, but sinners."

When Jesus was challenged about his disciples' failure to follow all the religious traditions of the day, Jesus called his accusers hypocrites: "You have let go of the commands of God and are holding on to the traditions of men."

On another occasion, his disciples argued about who was the greatest. Jesus confronted them and used the occasion to explain that whoever wanted to be first had to be last, and servant of all.

Some people claim that we do the same thing today with assertiveness training. Closer examination reveals, however, that much of it is designed simply to protect your rights and to make sure your position doesn't get challenged, damaged, or defamed. In other words, you learn how to stand up for what you have coming so no one can take it away from you.

That is not what we mean by confrontation, as practiced by Jesus. Confrontation deals not with the protection of your rights, but with the protection of your *values*. There is a major difference. I need to let God fight the battle of my personal rights. When my rights are challenged, God says I can hand over my defense to him; he will see to it that I'm protected. It is true that in the short term I may find myself facing "third down and forty yards to go" just to get back to the line of scrimmage, but God says he'll take care of me.

On the other hand, God encourages us to confront whenever our values are challenged. G.K. Chesterton once said, "I believe in getting into hot water; I think it keeps you clean." Some of us try to stay out of hot water at all costs. But there is danger in that. Our society lacks definition and intensity with regard to values because it doesn't like hot water. Hot water often means confrontation, and we try to avoid that. The theory goes like this: If you don't believe anything very deeply, you will never run into problems with people of opposing viewpoints. The more variable we are with our values, the less likely we are to confront.

I read recently about an Ivy League university that was given a $31 million grant to develop a business ethics program. The school is careful to make sure it doesn't suggest what those values should be; it simply teaches students how wonderful it is to have them. This university is spending $31 million to teach the value of values.

I suppose that's better than nothing. But to suggest there are no absolute values endangers society. Frankly, I'm glad that the American Revolution occurred two hundred years ago when people valued freedom. I'm not sure that today a majority would decide to cut the strings to Great Britain. I don't think we hold values deeply enough to want to protect them and to confront those who challenge them.

I believe that by protecting the values which define your life you will illuminate your world. Frankly, if there is nothing in your life worth dying for there is nothing in your life worth living for. You are left with a lackluster existence that has purposelessness written all over it.

In my experience, people long for something or someone they can believe in. They want it so badly, in fact, that they are capable of allying with losing teams in their rush to connect with something worth living for.

Alexander Hamilton wrote, "I'm sure that most of us looking back would admit that whatever we've achieved in character we've achieved through conflict." People who have become benchmarks of character, who have demonstrated the greatest personal achievement and progress, are people who have engaged in conflict when appropriate. They confronted the challenge to their fundamental values.

Recently, in Washington, D.C., a drama was played out through the courts, the penal system, and the congress. A woman refused to deliver her daughter to the family court, accepting instead a contempt charge that put her in jail for more than two years. The reason? She is convinced that her former husband has a history of child sexual abuse and is capable of abusing his own child. The judge did not agree, and Elizabeth Morgan demonstrated the depth of her resolve as she sat behind bars. Her fundamental commitment to her daughter was put to the test.

The greatest example of this courage to confront is Jesus of Nazareth. Let's return again to the case we examined earlier, where Jesus cleared out the money changers from the temple. Actually, he did this twice. His gentle demeanor throughout his three-year public ministry was bracketed by two violent events. As we examine the historical records, we can find insight on three points: when it is appropriate to publicly react; how to defend your values; and why such a defense is necessary.

When a defense is called for

The first reason for confronting faulty positions is to let the other side know you're there. A few years back, there was a great deal of talk about the "silent majority"—a large percentage of the populace that disagreed with societal trends but which remained mute because it didn't want to wade into the fray. Far from being a defense, this strategy is a passionless default of personal beliefs. It is this strategy that allows for an immoral minority to prevail over a superior (but apathetic) force.

The first cleansing of the temple was Jesus' first major public event. The previous events in his life occurred in isolated areas or in front of small crowds. The first thing Jesus did upon arriving in Jerusalem was to visit the temple. Now remember, there was no surprise here for Jesus. As God, he fully knew what was happening in the outer courtyard. The commercialization and desecration of the holy sanctuary had been a fact of life for years. The all-knowing Son of God walked into that situation with his eyes open and acted with forethought and resolve.

Jesus moved decisively to communicate a message. He was in town! He was a person to be reckoned with. He stood opposed to the goings-on. He was on the side of right. He did not clean house in his own name, but as an agent of his Father: "Take these things away; stop making My Father's house a house of merchandise."

Immediately afterwards, he became the target of hostile questions from the Jewish leaders. He captured their attention and opened the dialogue that would continue in the public arena for the next three years. So the first reason for a defense is to let the other side know you're there.

A second good reason for undertaking a defense of your values is that it may be necessary to establish an environment for pursuing your mission.

Suppose, for instance, that you are a school teacher in a public high school and your mission statement calls you to impart your faith in Jesus Christ to teenagers. In respect to your professional duties, you don't use your classroom to give your testimony. But you serve as an involved faculty sponsor for a student-initiated and student-led Christian club that meets on campus. In that setting, you are able to respond to interested students about your beliefs.

A parent whose child has never attended one of your meetings confronts the school administration with a demand to deny the use of classroom space to the club during nonschool hours, even though it meets all of the tests for sanctioned clubs imposed on any other group. The demand is based on the reasoning that such a club implies state establishment of religion and thus is unconstitutional. Should you, as a faculty member, put yourself in jeopardy by standing up for the club? It might be necessary to fulfill your mission.

Jesus found himself in such a position after three years of ministry. He landed back in Jerusalem during the Passover, and again set his sights on the temple. It was like an instant replay. I'm sure some of the money merchants sighed under their breath, "Here we go again!" as Jesus moved angrily through the ranks, causing pandemonium and chasing them out of the courtyard.

Now, Jesus had been in and out of Jerusalem during those three years. Yet he had not moved against these corrupters during those visits. Why, after all this time, would he again challenge their improper activities in the temple courts?

It certainly wasn't because he thought he could fix the problem. In a few days, he would be crucified. Seven weeks later he would return to heaven, his mission fulfilled. But the temple would be back to its former clutter and confusion. His cleansing was but a temporary respite from the trend toward unholiness.

So why was the Sunday of his last week spent sweeping out the dirt in the House of God? He was clearing the platform for his final presentation. During the next four days, he presented divine truth in this temple courtyard. Some of his most significant teaching occurred during this time, and we read that while the religious leaders were plotting to kill him, the crowd flocked to hear his teaching. Clearing the area provided the proper environment for pursuing his mission. Completing the work God had given him to do was primary. Jesus would do whatever was necessary to assure the satisfactory completion of that agenda.

How to mount a defense

This example might sound like a call for religious radicalism. Does this mean we are supposed to become Christian Rambos? Does the driven believer violate biblical principles and the laws of the land in pursuit of a godly objective? Some would think so.

Jesus, however, makes a great case for conscientious activism conducted with deliberate control. In every account of the cleansings, the record is the same: Jesus interrupted the status quo without abandoning his integrity. He drove the people out, but never abused them. He upset the merchandise without destroying it. He put them out of the temple, but not into the hospital. In his drive to respect God's property, he also respected their property. He wasn't against them; he was against what they were doing.

There is something unique about his approach, because his conduct didn't hinder his reception with the onlookers. Luke says that he cleaned out the merchandisers and then began to teach, reporting that the people "were hanging upon his words." That's the great test: you know you've responded incorrectly to the opposition when, as a result of your actions, you lose credibility rather than win it.

One Watergate participant whose prominence since the Nixon era has skyrocketed is Chuck Colson. Then Special Counsel to the President, Colson became a Christian just before serving time for his part in the Watergate scandal.

After his release, he founded Prison Fellowship, a ministry to prisoners around the world, and has become an outspoken advocate for penal reform in America and abroad.

With the eloquence of a politician and the credibility of a statesman, Colson boldly confronts the status quo as he appeals for a new approach to the growing prison populace. He goes head-to-head with the custodians of conventional wisdom in government as he calls for redemptive treatment for all.

Though at odds with his adversaries on this issue, he has won the respect of politicians and bureaucrats through his integrity and character. Though they may not agree with his position, they admire his commitment to the cause. He has successfully gained credibility, even when he hasn't gained adherents.

Why we need to defend the truth

The history of Christianity has been written around the life stories of men and women who could not be silenced. They were sure of what they believed and they were unstoppable in its proclamation.

Attacks on truth are not new. During the first century, church leader Jude urged Christians to "contend earnestly for the faith which was once for all delivered to the saints." The earliest protagonists varied in personality and temperament, but they agreed on strategy. Peter, the rough and tough fisherman, said he could not "stop speaking what we have seen and heard." Paul, the educated and erudite spokesman for the faith, found himself "reasoning daily" in settings as divergent as a hilltop meeting of Athenian philosophers and a synagogue of devout Jews in Asia.

Centuries later, Martin Luther put his life on the line when he nailed his ninety-five theses to the door of a church in Wittenberg, Germany. Martin Luther King, Jr., took his defense of racial equality to the point of death. Watchman Nee held fast to the truth of the gospel despite tortures and, eventually, martyrdom in a Chinese prison. The defenders of truth make up a mighty fraternity throughout history.

Managing Your Life

Is it better to defend truth or tolerate a lie? I have never seen a statue erected to the memory of heroic tolerance. I have seen them established to memorialize a love for truth, expressed to the point of great personal sacrifice.

Confrontation isn't necessary until you hold some values worth defending. One reason we acquiesce rather than confront is that we honor harmony over fuzzy values. In the space below, make a list of

your five most important values. Next to this list,
note the last time someone challenged those values.
What did you do? Did you confront the attack on
your basic values? If so, did you sense an inward satisfaction, or frustration in the encounter?

1.

2.

3.

4.

5.

CHAPTER TEN

Availability

While it's easy to dismiss mission-driven people as insensitive, no one ever did that with Jesus. He was deliberate about where he was going and what he was doing, but he also allowed himself to be detoured by needy people. Some men and women are so mission-oriented they forget people. Others are so people-oriented they forget mission. Jesus avoided both errors.

How can we strike a balance? We do so through the concept of availability.

It's appropriate that we consider this now after concentrating on such things as mission and control. Without balance, we can find ourselves growing depersonalized. The control-driven, mission-minded lifestyle must be complemented by the recognition that there are individuals with legitimate claims on our time and resources. Our objective is not to become so driven and intense that we become blind to these people, for people define our life.

How do we balance these conflicting principles? We do it by establishing an agenda, and using that agenda instead of serving a schedule. People who use an agenda will have time for those who require attention, even though they have no appointment. Some of the most important meetings in your day are not cataloged in your Daytimer.

I was knee-deep in deadlines one recent Friday, essentially checked-out so far as my staff were concerned. They were to consider me invisible to any demands that day—I could not be disturbed.

Even so, my secretary rang through to my office to tell me I had an urgent call. She gave me the name of the caller, and I didn't know her. I took the call anyway.

She sounded desperate and emotionally stretched. "No, you don't know me, but you would recognize my husband. We've really got to see you. Things are at a crisis point. We'll come anywhere. Just tell us what we have to do."

I looked at my schedule: there it was, lined-out for the day. I looked at my desk, piled high with past-due projects. I looked at my watch. The day was escaping while I was talking on the phone.

My schedule said no, but my agenda said yes. My agenda is people, not projects. My prime targets are hurting people with no other connections. I had ten reasons why I wasn't free, but none of them held up when confronted by someone who fit the profile for my life agenda.

They came to my office within the hour and stayed for three more. At the end of that time their marriage took a turn for the better—after two years of marital decline, punctuated by dramatic pitfalls and hurtful revelations. It was the best possible use of my day. Had I known about it in advance, I would have scheduled the meeting. Had I stuck to my schedule, I would have missed it.

What is the difference between agenda and schedule? An agenda is a program of things to be done. A schedule is a list of things to be done in a certain time frame.

It's the element of time that confuses us. We are so driven by the clock that the issues of timing and order become paramount—sometimes more important than the things that need to be done.

When we look at the life of Jesus, we are impressed that although he lived only thirty-three years and spent only three-and-a-half years in public ministry, at the time of his death he could say, "It is finished." He had completed the work he came to do. How could that be? The answer is found in his using an agenda rather than serving a schedule. In this way, he found time for those who required his attention, even though they came to him without an appointment. The same principle can work for us.

Let's look at three factors governing Jesus' availability, and how they apply to us today.

Take time to formalize your agenda

One of the most significant figures of the Reagan presidency may be a man who occupied a position that's normally out of the public eye. How many surgeons general can you name? Chances are, only the name of Dr. C. Everett Koop comes to mind.

What was it that burned his memory into the American consciousness? It was not primarily his military uniform or his odd gray beard, but rather his bold and controversial positions regarding smoking, AIDS, sex education, abortion, and other public health issues. Ironically, it was a period of personal humiliation that ultimately led to his success.

When Dr. Koop was nominated for surgeon general, he had to go through a laborious confirmation process by the Senate. His strong views led to vehement opposition from groups such as Planned Parenthood and the National Organization for Women. What was expected to be a quick confirmation turned into a nine-month battle.

For years, Dr. Koop had worked long hours as a world-renowned pediatric surgeon. Now, as he waited for Congress to complete its hearings, he had nothing to do. It was a frustrating situation for a man with enormous energy. Every day he went to a large but empty office and found nothing on his appointment calendar. What could he do with that time?

He found that this interlude was a wonderful gift—a time to think about the difference he could make as surgeon general. He developed plans for helping the cause of handicapped children, the elderly, battered women and children, and others in need. "During that nine months I developed a detailed agenda, something no surgeon general has ever had before," he said. "In the end, that period of acute frustration made possible every single thing I was able to accomplish in office. Now that's the sovereignty of God at work!"[1]

As a result of formalizing his agenda, Dr. Koop was not content to speak only when spoken to. He was unwilling to quiet the waters at all costs. He did not plan to speak softly and carry a big stick. He was not silenced by financial interests threatened by his ethically motivated pronouncements against unhealthful products.

As trustee of the national health, he set his agenda and pursued it tirelessly. He left office having made a mark on his world like no person in that position before him. He was proactive, not reactive. He set the cadence to which he marched.

That's what Jesus did. Soon after he began his public career at the age of thirty, Jesus returned home and attended the synagogue. There he was asked to be guest speaker. They handed him one of the sacred scrolls. He opened it and read the following from the prophet Isaiah: "The Spirit of the Lord is on me, because he has anointed me to preach good news to the poor. He has sent me to proclaim freedom for the prisoners and recovery of sight for the blind, to release the oppressed, to proclaim the year of the Lord's favor."

When he had finished reading, Jesus announced to the congregation, "Today this Scripture is fulfilled in your hearing." Jesus wanted his audience to understand that this was no random selection from the Bible. It was written six hundred to seven hundred years earlier to spell out his agenda . . . and it is exactly what he did.

That was his agenda. So the natural question arises, "How does agenda vary from purpose?"

Purpose is the rock-solid definition of direction in your life. Once you've determined why you're here, your purpose doesn't change. An agenda is the means by which, *for a period of time*, your purpose or mission is served. It is a list of things that have to be done to advance your mission.

Without an agenda, we quickly slip into a response mode. You arrive at the office every day and your activities are determined by your telephone calls and walk-ins. You do what seems appropriate in response to life. You respond instead of taking initiative.

I wager that people who are significant are rarely known as responders. It is people of initiative who go places and get things done. They have an agenda for life and work each day at implementing it. But agenda is just the first step. For it to work, we need to get more specific.

Develop a strategy to pursue your agenda

Soon after Jesus announced his agenda, he found himself swamped with people in Capernaum. He taught them, cast out demons, and healed the sick. He was doing what he said he would do. And he did it well enough that people wanted to invade his life. He was up late, but still managed to rise early the next morning and slip away to a lonely place. People went looking for him. They didn't want him to leave; they wanted him to preach some more, to continue what he had started.

But Jesus said, "I must preach the good news of the kingdom of God to the other towns also, because that is why I was sent." The people of

Capernaum said their strategy was to keep Jesus for themselves. They wanted him to perform his agenda there and only there. But Jesus rejected that idea. He said, "I'm taking my agenda all over. That's why I came." With his strategy so clear, he wasn't going to be distracted.

I try to use my vacation each year to do more than work on a tan. One thing I do is read the latest installment in my autobiography.

Whether you know it or not, you're writing an autobiography. You complete two chapters each year, both indisputably accurate. The journals that archive your life so irrefutably are your datebook and your checkbook. Show me those two records and I'll tell you your priorities, purpose, and agenda.

This year I reviewed my last twelve months through the window of my schedule . . . and was taken aback. My life showed a frightening trend. I was participating in multiple agendas at the expense of my own.

It didn't happen because I lacked an agenda. If you asked me, I could have rattled off my mission statement, my vision, my agenda, and my strategy, and you would have walked away impressed. Trouble was, my expression of that agenda was slipping, and nothing would change unless I did something about it.

Although I was in the last week of preparation for a much-needed three-week family vacation, I found myself parked in a restaurant booth, awaiting the arrival of a man I had never met. He had convinced me, through my secretary, that he really needed an hour of my day, and as I sat there I couldn't remember how he had managed that.

While I waited, I reviewed the prior month. My attention focused on the meals I had spent with people who had chased me—people selling something, people looking for career positions, people with no clear agenda who came recommended by some mutual acquaintance—people who had taken hour upon hour of my time, with no benefit ultimately gained for anyone.

I thought also about the guys I wanted to influence, but for whom I hadn't made time. These were the guys who didn't normally chase me for time, but who were ready when I had it available. No doubt their patience wore thin as I awaited yet another "blind date" lunch appointment.

It was another dud, but I gained from that lunch greatly. I flew back into my office afterward and sat down across the desk from my secretary. I handed her a list of fifty men with whom I wanted to spend time, and I asked her to call them while I was on vacation. When I returned, I had fifty appointments scheduled.

The best solution to my problem was to take control. I wouldn't have time to meet with the time-wasters because I would already be committed to the guys I really needed to be with.

What followed was one of the most fruitful quarters of the last five years. It was such a good move, I think I'll do it again!

Every hour in your day, every meeting you're in, every phone call you take either advances your agenda or someone else's. I try to measure how much of my time I am deliberately directing, and how much is falling prey to the demands of others. Last year, someone else was beating the drum, and I was marching.

I spent a couple of days rethinking my strategies for advancing my agenda. I asked myself what I needed to do, with whom I needed to spend time, how much I needed to be "unavailable." Then I carved those items into my future time frames.

Some relief has come since doing that exercise. But it remains a daily challenge to remain the director of my own God-honoring strategy rather than to become a pawn in some other person's plan for my life.

Now we're ready to deal with a most important concept. It has to do with interruptions, those unplanned and unscheduled moments that seem to throw you off course. They may not.

Allow your agenda to interrupt your schedule

Jesus allowed his agenda to supersede his schedule. Sometimes, when he had other things planned, he allowed people to interrupt. I'm convinced that most of us are willing to be available to the right people. They have instant access. But others don't get through your secretary. If they asked for an appointment, you would do anything necessary to dodge them.

And that may be okay. Most of us, however, probably do not make those decisions from the right value system. I know that when I look at Jesus. With him, the people who got through were the least likely ones. They were the ones our secretaries would probably screen. Let's look at several cases.

Once Jesus was leaving the city of Jericho, accompanied by his disciples and a large crowd. A blind man sat on the roadside, begging. When he heard that Jesus was passing by, he began to shout, "Jesus, Son of David, have mercy on me!" Many in the crowd rebuked the man and told him to be quiet. After all, he was an undesirable, a derelict. Useless. Why bother the master?

But Jesus stopped and ordered the crowd to call him. When they called the blind man he jumped to his feet and came to Jesus.

"What do you want me to do for you?" Jesus asked him.

"Rabbi, I want to see," the man replied.

"Then you have it!" Jesus answered. Immediately the man received his sight. While the crowd despised this man, Jesus took time for him and met his need.

On another occasion, Jesus was on his way to the home of a man named Jairus, whose daughter lay dying. Jairus was a ruler of the synagogue, a position of great influence. Time was of the essence, for the girl couldn't last much longer. Unfortunately, a traffic jam developed on the road. The bumper-to-bumper crowd nearly crushed Jesus.

In the midst of this mob stood a woman who for twelve years had suffered from hemorrhaging. No doctor had been able to heal her. In desperation, she touched the edge of Jesus' cloak; instantly she was healed.

Jesus could have kept right on going; after all, he was in a hurry, and the woman no doubt would have preferred anonymity. It's hard to imagine that Jesus even noticed this particular touch in the jostling crowd anyway. But he stopped and asked "Who touched me?" The woman was scared. But when she saw that Jesus wouldn't leave until she identified herself, she came trembling and fell at his feet to explain why she had touched him and how she had been instantly healed.

It's important to understand the significance of this encounter. Her condition made her an outcast— the possibility of infecting others meant she could have no contact with society. In the Jewish vernacular, she was considered "unclean."

And here is Jesus, rushing to his most important meeting of the day, stopping to talk to one of the most undesirable people of that time. He's instantly available to a woman who has no entree to the rest of society. The least likely person has his full attention, and he solves her problem.

The situation soon becomes even more complicated. While Jesus is delayed, Jairus's daughter dies and his servants arrive to relay the news—it won't be necessary to trouble Jesus any further. But Jesus isn't ignoring the need of Jairus. Just as he met the need of this poor woman, he will meet the need of the synagogue ruler. He continues on to the ruler's home and raises the little girl from the dead.

A third example of Jesus' availability came in his encounter with a traitorous tax man. (Some of you may think those terms are synonymous and redundant!) Jesus was passing through Jericho again. In that city lived a man named Zacchaeus, a chief tax collector and a wealthy man. Because he was short, he couldn't see Jesus through the crowd so he ran ahead and climbed a tree. When Jesus reached that spot, he looked up at Zacchaeus and said, "Come down immediately. I must stay at your house today."

Taxes in that day were like MacDonald's—they were franchised. You bid for a tax district to the

Roman government and agreed to pay a certain rate. Anything you collected over and above that, you could keep. Not a bad way to get rich, you say? True; but for a Jew, it also meant being ostracized by your community. Zacchaeus's own people considered him a traitor. Why would anyone want to be seen with this man?

Well, there was one who did—Jesus. He interrupted his trip through town to eat dinner with Zacchaeus. When no one else would talk to this man, Jesus did. As a result, Zacchaeus's life was changed. He promised to pay back all those he'd cheated and to give half of all he owned to the poor. Jesus said, "Today salvation has come to this house."

There is a stark contrast between the questions, "Where are you supposed to be?" and "What are you trying to accomplish?" Sometimes we can focus too much on the first and not at all on the second.

Years ago, Dr. Billy Graham was engaged in a series of meetings in the Northeast. He was having a significant impact on thousands of people. The leaders and churches involved in hosting the meetings implored Dr. Graham to extend his time with them to take advantage of what God was doing in their midst.

Billy's schedule did not allow him to say yes to their request. A series of crusade meetings had been planned in Canada, scheduled to begin just as the Northeast meetings were reaching their zenith. Billy left the certain moving of God's Spirit in the Northeast for the possibility of the Spirit's movement at meetings not yet begun.

Dr. Graham later reported that this was one of the most obvious mistakes of his career. His schedule was deemed more important than his agenda. God never arrived at the Canadian meetings in the way he had been apparent in America. The evangelist had kept his appointments at the expense of his mission.

Managing Your Life

There are times when interrupting a man-made schedule is the right thing to do in view of a God-ordained agenda. Your schedule is capable of disabling your agenda and destroying your effectiveness. Take a few minutes to list five things that warrant top billing on your agenda:

1.

2.

3.

4.

5.

After making this list, find a spot in your day planner to jot these as a reminder. When you are faced with an opportunity to serve that agenda this week, do it, even if you lose ground in your schedule.

(Note—This applies to the portion of our schedule that is within our control; everyone has varying degrees of binding commitment to something outside their control. Focus on the aspects on which you call the shots.)

1. Philip D. Yancey, "The Embattled Career of Dr. Koop," *Christianity Today,* October 20, 1989, p. 18.

CHAPTER ELEVEN

Focus

You've set your agenda. But now the intrusions arrive via the telephone, mail, and walk-ins. Hard as you try, you can't seem to stop these distractions from draining your energy. You're not as effective as you should be.

Some people think this is a *good* strategy. "Spread the risk," they say. "You never know what might work, so diversify." That may be a good investment strategy, but it's a disaster for personal success. To really make your energy count the most, you have to focus that energy on your mission.

In 1980, a thirteen-year-old California girl was killed in a car accident by a repeat DWI offender.

Her mother, enraged at the leniency of the laws and judicial system toward drunk-driving cases, directed her energies toward changing her society's position on drinking and driving.

In the next ten years, Gloria Leitner mobilized America under the Mothers Against Drunk Driving (MADD) banner. Now more than 1.1 million supporters strong, they continue their march toward putting a final end to tragedies caused by alcohol-and-drug-impaired driving. This group's groundswell of passionate activity has resulted in an astounding 97 percent name recognition among American adults. Annual deaths from drinking and driving have fallen during this period, and 390 local chapters nationwide have provided effective lobbying to shape the legislative response to this problem. Educational programs aimed at prevention are now a major thrust of MADD's multi-pronged initiative. Truly, Leitner's focus on a tragic issue has helped change her world.

I maintain that Gloria Leitner achieved her impact through an ability to focus. By narrowing her target and her objective, she succeeded in a critical area of life. So can you. Doesn't that have more appeal than sitting in your Lazy-Boy and mailing in your monthly dues to the Flabby Fraternity of the Mediocre?

It's been said that no horse goes anywhere until he's harnessed; no steam drives anything until it's confined; no river generates any electricity until its channeled. Likewise, no life ever grows great until it is focused, dedicated, and disciplined.

Many men and women fail to leave a legacy of effective influence because they do not concentrate their energies and talents into any specific area. On the other hand, the greatest figures of history all knew how to focus. Having defined their mission, they gave themselves fully to the enterprise.

Consider how this was true in the life of Jesus Christ. His three-and-a-half years of public ministry were highly focused, and the way he fixed his attention gives us insight into how we can focus.

Determine the identity of your natural market

First, notice that Jesus focused on a specific audience. He wasn't out to talk to the whole world. One time he visited the region of Tyre and Sidon and a Canaanite woman came to him. Her daughter was suffering terribly from demon possession and she begged Jesus for help.

Now, Jesus did help her—he demonstrated the balance between focus and availability—but before he did, he made this statement: "I was sent only to the lost sheep of Israel." Jesus made an exception in this case, but he wasn't going to be diverted from proclaiming his message to the Jews.

Did that mean he didn't have compassion for non-Jewish people? Not at all. But his intent was to focus on one group, and to train a few people within that group. Later, after he returned to heaven, his followers would take his message to the world.

Jesus also focused within his target group. Early in his ministry, he befriended a tax collector named Matthew. Matthew was so thrilled that he invited all of his tax collector friends to his house to meet Jesus. This deeply offended the religious types, who complained to those who followed Jesus around.

Jesus didn't ignore their complaint. He answered, "It is not the healthy who need a doctor, but the sick. I have not come to call the righteous, but sinners to repentance." In other words, Jesus identified two kinds of folk within his broad target market: those who didn't believe they had any needs, and those who didn't have any doubt that they did. Jesus said "I've only got three-and-a-half years to work the territory. I'm not going to waste my time trying to convince people who think they've got it all together. I'm going to the people who know they need what I've got."

I spend my life working among a distinctive group of people. Demographers have given them the name Baby Boomers—those born in the U.S. between the years 1946 and 1964. I relate to Boomers because I am one. We were raised on Hostess Cupcakes and Ozzie and Harriet. We watched the Rose Parade and the Viet Nam War from our living rooms in living color. We got more schooling, better jobs, and higher salaries than the generation before us.

But I also relate to a sub-group of Boomers, the Yuppies. That's a term losing its attractiveness, but descriptive nonetheless. I speak their language. I know their thought processes. I communicate best to Yuppie Boomers; they are my best market.

A couple of years ago, a friend invited me to speak at a New Year's weekend retreat for high schoolers. My friend had heard me do events like that for adults and thought I'd do a great job with these kids. Boy, was he wrong! There were two hundred of them, and one of me. I couldn't connect with them for anything. Nothing worked. My silver tongue turned to tin. My humor came up moronic. The things that excite Boomers drove these boys and girls up the wall. I was out of my element.

Another time I spent a week two thousand miles from home speaking to a group of senior citizens from the agricultural communities of the heartland. Wonderful people—but I didn't know the first thing about their world. I could have used a translator. That week was the longest week of my life. I was convinced again that my primary market is very narrow and that I ignore it at my own peril.

If you are most effective with a particular, identifiable type or group of people, doesn't it make sense to spend the majority of your time with them? I know folks who make up their mind to talk to whomever calls. I'm convinced that if your schedule is filled primarily with people who have asked to see you, you're probably unfocused and ineffective.

Now, Jesus certainly was available to those occasional people who came to him even though they were not within his target market. But they weren't his priority. Jesus knew his primary audience, a very narrow band of people.

Develop the essence of your central message

President Franklin D. Roosevelt was once asked how long it would take to prepare an address on a particular theme. "That depends on how long you want me to speak," the President answered. "If you want an hour on the issue, I can be ready in two days. If you want thirty minutes, it will take me a week. If you want five minutes, it may take a month to prepare." FDR knew that arriving at the essence is one of the most demanding of all exercises.

Great people in history are often remembered because of their ability to express their life message, and to do it often. Winston Churchill was announced as the speaker for a public meeting. The full text of his address was: "Never give up. Never give up! Never, never, never give up!"

Abraham Lincoln is memorialized not for the hundreds of orations he delivered over a public life that spanned three decades, but for a thoughtful speech of less than two hundred words. It's called The Gettysburg Address.

Jesus demonstrated his focus in a concise message, which one of the gospel writers recorded like this: "The time has come. The kingdom of God is near. Repent and believe the good news!"

First, Jesus established the immediate importance of his message. Second, he delivered the heart of his message—"The kingdom of God is before you, embodied in me." And third, he gave a solid close— "Here's what you need to do."

Have you noticed that successful candidates for political office are often those who are able to communicate one point clearly? Challenger Ronald Reagan scored a TKO over incumbent Jimmy Carter in the 1980 presidential debates by asking one simple question: "Are you better off now than you were four years ago?"

We've all had to endure people who take hours of our time filling the air with 200 words a minute, gusts up to 550. When they're finished, we can't remember anything they said.

What would your friends say is your message? Do they say, "Beats me, but he's a nice guy." Well, my dog's nice, too. We need to think about the message we want to leave behind. What is it that you believe in and want to communicate so badly that you are willing to reduce it to an understandable core?

Realize the expedience of a limited time frame

Everyone works within a limited time frame. You are playing out the finite number of days assigned to you, and it may be this very ticking of the clock that will encourage you to make something happen.

In 1972, Ara Parseghian brought his Fighting Irish football team from South Bend, Indiana, to the Los Angeles Coliseum for the final game of the regular season. His opponent was the USC Trojans, a Notre Dame rival for forty-eight years. Though the Trojans were favored by four points, the Irish had been rated the top defensive team in the nation. The stage was set for a game well worth the price of admission.

The contest began in a familiar pattern as the Irish pulled out in front with some unexpected play-action passes. By halftime, the score stood in Notre Dame's favor, 24-6. It looked like an easy win for the Irish.

Then came seventeen minutes of agony for Ara Parseghian and the Fighting Irish. The 84,000 spectators at the Coliseum, and millions watching by television, saw the Trojan offensive and defensive units explode to life. In those seventeen minutes, USC scored 49 points, almost at will.

Tony Davis opened the second half with a remarkable 102-yard touchdown sprint through the entire Irish defense. A few plays later he scored again. Pat Haden took care of whatever Tony Davis left undone. By the time the dust settled in the southern California twilight, the scoreboard told the electrifying tale: USC, 55; Notre Dame, 24.

A limited time frame will either immobilize a

person in fear or energize him in expectancy. For USC, it did the latter. The Trojans' sense of urgency propelled them to extraordinary performance.

Imagine that this morning, an associate at your office pulled you aside and said, "You just received a FAX. God called and wanted you to know that you've only got three-and-a-half years left, and that's it. Thought you'd like to know." How would you react?

Jesus held a strong sense of the limited time he had to accomplish his mission. He began his public work at age thirty. About a year-and-a-half to two years later, he drew twelve men to himself and began to spend concentrated time with them, explaining that he had to go to Jerusalem and suffer many things. He even told them that he would be killed and that he would be raised to life again three days later. At the age of thirty-two, he heard the clock ticking. He knew he was running out of time.

On the night before he was killed, Jesus offered a marvelous prayer. He began it by saying that the time had come, that he had finished the work God gave him to do. No lament about a job missed; no regret that time ran out before he could complete all of his tasks. Just a simple, matter-of-fact statement that his work was through.

If you knew you had only forty-two months left, would you be more focused than you are today? Most of us have a deep-seated sense of immortality. We live out our lives as if we had all the time in the world . . . but we don't. Statistically, the odds are high that someone reading this book has no more than three-and-a-half years left. The more we realize our time limits, the more convinced we become of the need to focus.

Understand the significance of your personal responsibility

Most everything I needed to know in life I learned in high school football. My team was a melting pot of ethnic flavors, coached by a similarly broad mix of committed men. My mentor was a 6' 5" 260-pound persuader named Manny Penaflor.

As the giant on the defensive line (I weighed in at 172 pounds, minus gear), Manny would often start with me when demonstrating a point. One day as we lined up for scrimmage, Manny decided to capture a teaching opportunity. He had a peculiar way of seizing our attention—he grabbed your face mask and pulled you up real close, so you wouldn't miss a single word.

On this particular day, he grabbed my face mask and yelled in his distinctive accent, "Chank, you're a defensive tackle, not the whole team. I don't want you playing the whole field. Here's your job."

He let me go and used his foot to scratch a ten-foot by ten-foot square around my spot on the line. "Chank, you see this square?" I couldn't miss it. "This square is yours. Anybody from the other team who comes into this square, it's your job to put them on their butt. You got that?"

When he was convinced I understood my assignment, he moved to the middle guard, Ernie Norton, and went through the same theatrics. Property rights were assigned in 100-square-foot increments to five linemen and two linebackers. None of us could ever say we didn't know what was expected of us. We knew our personal responsibilities.

I think of Manny often when I tense up over what needs to be done on a global scale. I have a tendency to become frustrated, then fatalistic, because I can't get my arms around all there is to do. It's at those moments that I need to remember I'm not assigned the whole planet. I've only been entrusted with a particular slice of it. That is the portion of the world for which God will one day hold me accountable.

Jesus knew his area of personal responsibility. He stated it clearly when he addressed a large crowd: "I have come down from heaven not to do my will but to do the will of him who sent me." He also said he would welcome everyone whom God would give him.

At this point, there's a great temptation to read this as yet another goal-setting challenge. That is definitely *not* the point. Goals presume that you and I can decide what the future will be. Perhaps you've attended those seminars where you're challenged to "just name what you're going to sell, and how much income you're going to draw next year. You have the power to speak it into existence." That is a lie.

An exceptionally wise man of history named Solomon said at the peak of his career: "Man rolls the dice; God determines the outcome." Was he right? When he was an old man, looking back at life with the voice of experience, he said, "The race is not always to the swift. The battle does not always go to the strong. Success does not always come to the wise." God says we can't figure out the future.

Jesus did not come to earth for "results." He came to do what God told him to do. These were the results: "All that the Father gives me will come to me." The results were in God's hands.

Unfortunately, I meet people every day who are

committed to results and will do anything to get them. God will never ask you, "What did you achieve?" He'll ask "Did you serve me?" He will ask, "Were you faithful?" Jesus said, "Those who come to me—that's up to God. What happens when they come to me—that's my responsibility; I will never drive them away."

Many people consider their lives upside down because they don't see results. I often ask, "Are you doing what God wants you to do?" Sometimes they say, "Yes, but it's not working." I tell them, "Yes it is. It may not accomplish what you expected—God never said it would. He only said it's what he wants you to do."

When Manny drew that 100-square-foot box for me, he said my responsibility was to knock down any enemy player who dared enter. The opposition might score a touchdown around the opposite end, but I couldn't do anything about that. He wouldn't criticize me for it as long as I did my job.

Managing Your Life

You may be thinking that you should broaden your life rather than narrow your focus. Realize that your effectiveness will increase when you focus. Take a minute to write down your own focus in each of the four areas we've covered:

SPECIFIC AUDIENCE:

CONCISE MESSAGE:

FINITE TIME FRAME:

PERSONAL RESPONSIBILITY:

Are you satisfied with what you observe in each area? Is your effectiveness heightened or minimized by your current status? What do you need to do to narrow your focus in the out-of-focus areas?

CHAPTER TWELVE

Excellence

I've grown to love one of the genuine statesmen of the Christian kingdom. His name is Fred
Smith, Sr., a man whose business experience spans
the bulk of the twentieth century. He has served on
more corporate boards than most people can list and
speaks all over the world. But for me, what attracts
me to Fred is his wisdom.

As a young boy, Fred cut his right hand on a
broken mason jar. An inept country doctor mis-
treated the injury, rendering Fred's hand nearly unus-
able. Fred's perspective on his hand has more power
than any healthy fist could equal. "You see this hand?
This is all I can do with it," he tells a spellbound

audience. "But let me tell you something. This hand is not my problem. It's a fact of life. Do you know the difference? A problem is something you can do something about. There's nothing I can do about my hand. A fact of life is something you can't change. So you accept that and get on with your life."

Fred is a wonderful role model of the pursuit of excellence. I've heard him say, "I get so tired of hearing people tell me about the problems that hold them back from achieving what they want to achieve in life. Truth is, most of them are confused. They've confused their facts of life with problems. They think they can fix something that can't be fixed, and they're stifled by problems that deny them their future."

This is the final element in our Total Life Management package. By performing to your full potential, you will exceed the expectations of those who live to minimize others.

Many of these folks have a tremendous desire to regularly remind you that you will never be much more than you are today. They aim to keep you from realizing what you could really be. People who are excellent do not necessarily win the accolades of their contemporaries.

What we want to discover is the often unappreciated potential in each of us. And we'll see that there is one whose approval and acclaim we *can* live for, someone who wants us to become all that we were created to be.

Unfortunately, most of us are driven by the bell-curve mentality. We generally are most comfortable within the heart of the bell, where 90 percent of the population resides. When we start moving toward the outer limits, we make people uncomfortable.

Early in my business life, I was given the opportunity to transfer from an administrative support role in the purchasing department to a newly created position in the sales department. The company specialized in securing six-figure contracts with clients in the home-building industry, but my field of responsibility was to take our product directly to the retail buyer, with sales averaging about 3 percent of the company's normal take in its primary market. Simply stated: it took thirty-three "deals" from my department to equal one "deal" from the other departments. I was no threat to my older, wiser cohorts.

That is, I didn't appear to be a threat. Over the next year, my field of opportunity blossomed. No one had considered that the profit percentage potential of my sales might exceed that of the large-scale contracts. It turned out that the company made more money on fifteen of my sales than it did on one of the larger contracts. Within twelve months, the profit contribution from my activities was greater than that of any other sales executive in the firm—some of whom had been in the industry for longer than I had been alive! The department that had been slighted by the veterans was now getting noticed!

How did they react to my unexpected success? If you're guessing celebrations were convened in my honor, think again. Rather than plaques and back-slaps, my team began to receive scrutiny and back-stabs. This dark-horse addition to the company stable threatened the long-time teammates. Their security was challenged by the presence of a young, lightly trained co-worker who had found a way to produce.

You don't always win friends when you win.

Only the man who excels has to answer the criticisms of those who challenge competence. The perfect example of this is Jesus Christ. Although he was popular, he faced plenty of criticism from religious and political leaders and former followers who expected a different kind of Messiah. But criticism and unpopularity never stopped Jesus from pursuing excellence in all he did. Let's see how his example can be a model for us.

Aspire to deliver an exemplary performance

Jesus visited Capernaum early in his ministry and spoke at the local synagogue on the Sabbath. The people were amazed by his teaching—he didn't teach like the trained teachers of the law. "He taught them as one who had authority," says the Bible.

Religious teachers at that time spent years learning about the law and studying commentaries on it. These guys had a corner on the market. They were organized: "Teachers of the Law, Local 425"—dues-paying members of the public communicator club. People had become used to their droning performances, and public expectations were low. Then here comes an unknown from the little borough of Nazareth. He lands in the middle of this scene and begins to communicate. The people wake up, take notice, and realize how different this is from the normal chatter.

The religious leaders didn't take too kindly to this newcomer, and for several reasons. First, the religious leadership in that society was strictly upper crust; only a certain pedigree allowed you to break into that group. Your family had to spring from the tribe of Levi, the group entrusted with the priesthood some fifteen centuries before. The problem was that Jesus hailed from the tribe of Judah—known for its prominent political leaders, not its spiritual leaders. He didn't fit the accepted criteria for a spiritual authority.

Second, everyone knew that teachers needed to have formal training. The foremost religious educator of his day was a man named Gamaliel, whose students learned at his feet in the Temple training institute. Among his notable students in the first century was a man named Saul of Tarsus, a Pharisee of some distinction. On the other hand, among those who had never seen the inside of the Temple training institute was Jesus, a carpenter from Nazareth. Claiming no acceptable rabbi as his mentor, Jesus came to the party with no recognized alma mater. He was no easy player to evaluate: you couldn't judge him from his résumé (he didn't have one). You were forced to evaluate him on his own merits, something his critics were unprepared to do.

A friend of mine is the CEO of one of the largest firms in his industry. He supervises a staff of nearly two hundred people and oversees business activity measured in the hundreds of millions of dollars annually. This guy is a winner at what he does. Not only is his company highly profitable, but he serves in the senior leadership of the trade association that involves all of his competitive peers.

Recently, he had a breakfast meeting with three yuppie bankers striving to win his company's business. During the course of their table talk they began swapping stories about their experiences in business school. As the bankers compared pedigrees and alma maters, they turned to my friend and asked him where he got his MBA. "I don't have an MBA," he answered.

Naturally, they asked him where he did his undergraduate work. My friend leaned forward, as if to share a secret. Then he dropped this bombshell: "I didn't go to college."

Dumb luck arrived about that time. I walked into the restaurant while this conversation was in progress. At the moment the bankers' jaws fell on the table, I saw my buddy and came over to greet him. He told me later that if I hadn't interrupted them at that moment, they might still be fumbling for a response.

What was the problem? The bankers couldn't reconcile this man's exemplary accomplishments with his rudimentary résumé. A truck had just run over all their tidy assumptions about the prerequisites for professional achievement.

Wouldn't it be tragic if you decided that your future was limited by your past? Some people would tell my high school graduate friend that his lack of college would keep him from responsible management positions. But his background is not his problem; it's just a fact of life. He accepted it long ago. He demonstrates that our past doesn't need to limit us in pursuing our mission.

My friend was prepared for life even though he didn't go through all the "right" training programs. I've seen college graduates who aren't prepared, and I've found people who are prepared who never attended college. The question shouldn't be "Where did you go to school?" but rather, "Are you educated?"

Jesus wasn't formally educated in the schools where the Pharisees got their theological degrees. But he was thoroughly prepared.

If you have a dream that doesn't make sense to anyone but you, don't let the doomsayers near it. Protect it. Nurture it. Commit it to the Creator of every dream that honors him, and give the rest of your life to turning it into reality.

In the process, expect to be criticized. People won't understand what you are doing and will attack you. Count on it.

Anticipate the criticism of the ever-present detractors

In case it hasn't dawned on you, the world is not standing on the sidelines cheering you to victory. In fact, they're usually on the opposing side of the field whooping it up when you get tackled for a loss. Sometimes you get the feeling that public opinion runs the direction of universal antagonism—people don't seem to want anyone to win. If someone starts to shine, the goal is to tarnish him as quickly as possible.

You don't serve long in the role of an aspiring world-changer before you run into sniper fire. Jesus sure experienced it. Shortly after his powerful performance in Capernaum, he started getting flak from different pockets of his peer group. Let's look at some of the groups that attacked him.

Family

This might surprise you. We tend to have this nice, traditional picture of Mary and Joseph and their wonderful little family. We can almost see them gathering for the holidays with never a hint of dissension. What a warm, embracing, self-worth affirming group!

Well, not exactly. When Jesus started speaking in public, his family recoiled. In fact, once he spoke in a house, and the crowd grew so great that the disciples couldn't even eat. When his family heard about it, they decided to go and take charge of him because, they said, "He is out of his mind."

This sounds like the dark side of the Brady Bunch. Jesus had become a family embarrassment. How could they let him run loose? What would the neighbors think? How would they explain to their friends at the synagogue? The situation required decisive action.

So they went to get him. On arrival, they sent a message to the front of the crowd—"your family is outside looking for you." And how did Jesus respond? He looked at those around him and said, "This is my family!" Jesus made it clear that his family didn't consist of people who shared a DNA chain with him. Rather, it consisted of those who shared with him a common ideology.

Jesus' family grew troubled that he was performing at a level beyond their comfort zone. I don't think they were unusual. Family can be our best supporters. But all too often, when we step out and do something different, family doesn't understand. And usually when they don't understand, they try to pull us down to a more comfortable level.

Community

Shortly after this encounter with his family, Jesus did visit his hometown. On the Sabbath, he again went into the synagogue to teach. And again, the people who heard him were amazed. Then they started analyzing what they had seen and heard. "Where did this man get these things? What's this wisdom that has been given him, that he even does miracles? Isn't this the carpenter? Isn't this Mary's son and the brother of James, Joseph, Judas, and Simon? Aren't his sisters here with us?" And they took offense at him.

Look how quickly they moved from amazement to offense. What happened in that short time? The crowd began to chatter. And what did they chatter about? They questioned how this man, who was one of them, got his "stuff." They didn't ask if it was valid. They assumed it wasn't because it was unconventional. Jesus didn't go to college. He didn't have the right job. He didn't have the right family background. It just wasn't what they expected. So they assumed he was wrong.

It was then that Jesus uttered those oft-quoted words:

"Only in his hometown and in his own house is a prophet without honor."

Are there exceptions? Yes. But many have felt what he felt that day. There's no harder crowd to win over than the folks who knew you when, and who think they know why your current effectiveness may not last. It's hard for many people to watch a neighbor succeed and wish him well . . . in fact, it's often the motivation to launch an attack that might pull them back down to the mean once again.

Leaders

Jesus encountered resistance from a third area—the religious and political elite. Of all the groups we've looked at, it makes sense that these folks should be the most offended, for Jesus challenged their power base. Still, their methods of attack might surprise us. One time they came up to Jesus and said, "Aren't we right in saying that you are a Samaritan and demon-possessed?"

Think of the worst ethnic slur possible, and that's what these people used. They called Jesus a half-breed. They said he was worthless and demon-possessed. They used the most outrageous epithets to put him down.

It was so blatant that Jesus couldn't ignore all of it. He passed over the ethnic slur, but he addressed the question of his spiritual identity: "I am not possessed by a demon, but I honor my Father and you dishonor me." The leaders shot back, "We know that you are demon-possessed," and added, "Who do you think you are?"

Who do you think you are? Only eternity will reveal how many people faded from view, their potential unrealized, because of this simple phrase. We probably can all look back and find wounds inflicted by those who were threatened when we tried to fulfill our potential. Perhaps they feared an out-of-control ego, or an unwillingness to be "normal." Maybe they thought us out of step with reality. If we listened to them, we climbed back into the same miry pit of mediocrity that ensnares most people.

Based on the opposition he received from family, community, and leadership, it's amazing we ever heard of Jesus. If we listened to the majority voices, we'd have to believe he couldn't go anywhere, that we'd never hear any more from him. But in fact, the opposite happens. From the time of these denunciations until the end of his life, we find that he performed more and more beyond their expectations. Even within his lifetime, vindication came.

Await the vindication of the final appraisal

Some homespun sage put it bluntly: "It ain't over till it's over." Excellence isn't a snapshot; it is the epilogue for the mission-driven person who has persevered to the end.

A great figure of history illustrates this truth well. His mother died at an early age. His formal education was minimal. At twenty-two his first business failed. Like many who fail in business, he decided to run for political office. At age twenty-three he lost the race for a local office. At age twenty-four, he started another business and failed again. Fortunately, the next year he was elected to the state legislature. During his term, his fiancée died.

At age twenty-seven, he suffered a nervous breakdown. At twenty-nine, he ran for speaker of the house and was defeated. At thirty-one, he ran for a state elector and lost. At thirty-four, he ran for Congress and lost. But he didn't quit. He ran again two years later, and at age thirty-seven he was elected. Two years later, however, he was defeated in a bid for re-election.

Talk about a mid-life crisis! By age forty, this man had experienced two business failures, death of a loved one, a nervous breakdown, and several election defeats. And it got worse. At age forty-six, he ran for Senate and lost. A year later, he was listed on the party ticket as candidate for vice-president. The ticket lost. At forty-nine, he lost another race for Senate.

Time to place your bets on his life. What do you think? Is he a winner or a loser? Should he fade from view and accept his mediocrity? Is he just a dreamer with delusions of grandeur? What would you counsel him to do with his life?

Last year I was riding in the top deck of a double-decker bus in London, taking in a one-day tour of the city before my flight from Heathrow Airport. As we rounded a corner in downtown London, our guide pulled alongside a bronze statue standing in the middle of a traffic circle. Guess who it was? The very man who had made it a habit to lose in his pursuit of a life mission—Abraham Lincoln.

I'm glad Lincoln didn't give up his dream. At the age of fifty-one, he was elected President of the United States and led this country during its most crucial test. Had he folded his tent and gone home rather than press on, the future of the world might well have been altered. Instead, throughout the world he is regarded as one of our greatest statesmen.

Jesus was vindicated even during his lifetime. Look at his final appraisal, first from his competitors—the men who vied for the affection and attention of the community. They sent a delegation to him. Though they were trying to trap him, they recognized who he was: "Teacher, we know you are a man of integrity. You aren't swayed by men, because you pay no attention to who they are; but you teach the way of God in accordance with the truth." His enemies still didn't like him, but they had to admit the obvious—"You've gone far beyond what we ever thought you could do." I don't think these men ever spoke any harder words.

It's interesting also to see what happened to the man who stood in judgment over Jesus—Pilate. His role in the execution of Jesus was curious. He admitted to the religious leaders, "You brought me this man as one who was inciting the people to rebellion. I have examined him in your presence and have found no basis for your charges against him." Pilate then sent Jesus to Herod, the titular king of the Jewish people, and not even Herod could find anything against Jesus.

This was like unleashing the Washington press corps on one guy and saying, "Call every deepthroat informant you know and tell him to spill his guts on Jesus." They followed him, they photographed him, they quizzed people, and still they couldn't find anything amiss. The execution of Jesus was purely a political act; there was no basis for it in fact.

Jesus also was vindicated by his followers. You would think if there was any dirt on Jesus, it would be known to those closest to him. Certainly the "kiss and tell" phenomenon is not new. But the man closest to him, John, had nothing to say against him, and neither did any of his other followers. In fact, they concluded he was God!

I am overwhelmed by the example of Jesus Christ. In his life, he established a stimulating example that can influence the way you and I live today. He showed it in the way he pursued excellence. He showed us that excellence is not an objective standard set by some human committee. Excellence goes beyond what people are prepared to see in your life. Whatever limitation the world wants to impose, it can be overcome when we pursue a God-ordained mission.

Managing Your Life

People want to be able to explain away excellence by pointing to education or upbringing or circumstances as the reason for personal achievement. Excellence hinges on escaping the limiting expectations of those around you.

Evaluate on a ten-point scale what kind of performance most people expect from you because of your résumé:

1—2—3—4—5—6—7—8—9—10

On the same scale, how would you currently rate your overall performance in life?

1—2—3—4—5—6—7—8—9—10

Also on a ten-point scale, what do you know your potential to be when considering the magnifying factor of God in your life?

1—2—3—4—5—6—7—8—9—10

Finally, what is one thing you can do now to move the number on the second scale closer to the number on the third scale?

At this moment, you may be one decision short of a significant breakthrough in your life. You may be reviewing a checkered past, wondering if it isn't masochistic to keep chasing your vision. Your head is pounding a cadence that your heart finds increasingly difficult to step to. How long do you have to wait to be rewarded?

For me, it helps to remember a dank dungeon cell and a prisoner awaiting execution. This man had time to write one last letter to a young friend a continent away. Some would say this prisoner had been a fool—a man whose prominence and promise were scrapped decades earlier in favor of an unpopular cause. He had given his prime years to recruit men and women to a radical message of transformation made possible by an obscure Hebrew carpenter. The writer, whom we know as Paul the Apostle, gave his young protégé Timothy the encouragement you may need today to "go for it":

> The time has come for me to leave this life. I have fought the good fight. I have finished the race. I have kept the faith. Now a crown is waiting for me. I will get that crown for being right with God. The Lord is the judge who judges rightly, and he will give me the crown on that day. He will give that crown not only to me but to those who have waited with love for him to come again.
>
> (2 Timothy 4:6b-8, The Everyday Bible [New Century Version]).

Epilogue

This book has been woven from two very different life stories. One is the story of my life.

My textbook "Type A" lifestyle was radically reoriented more than ten years ago by a life-purpose statement. Since that time, I have used that statement as a compass to direct my life. During that time, I have discovered two amazing things.

The first is that Cheri and I have made some radical shifts in our lives. In 1981, I left a secure executive position with a multinational corporation to start my own business. Though most entrepreneurial ventures are motivated by the founder's desire to advance professionally or financially, my decision was made to maintain freedom and flexibility to pursue my purpose statement. The clearest affirmation for this move came from our purpose statement; it was, at that point in our lives, the best means for us to advance our mission.

In 1984, I sold my business and founded Priority Living, a non-profit organization designed to serve business and professional men and women. Can you guess the purpose of our ministry?

"Priority Living exists to cause biblical life change in business and professional men and women through teaching the timeless word of God in a contemporary context."

I enjoy the greatest of all setups: I am the CEO of an organization whose purpose mirrors my own!

When asked how we managed to make two potentially stress-laden decisions of this magnitude within five years, I point to our purpose statement. Choosing the course that best advanced our mission made these decisions clear.

After moving through seasons of a career cycle that often result in mid-life crisis, I have seen the value of a stable benchmark against which to measure our activities and commitments. As a couple, Cheri and I are planning for the upcoming phases of our lives and are anticipating great things as we pass from one season to the next.

My second discovery during the 1980s is that we represent a tiny minority. Most men and women have never thought through the question of their purpose in life.

It is possible that you may be one of those who has never put on paper your vision for life. If we have the occasion to meet in the future, it would be my hope to hear that you accepted the challenge to think this subject through to a conclusion. Living on purpose is the only way to go!

Much of this book has been about my experiences. To be honest, you can take my experiences or leave them—but the same is not true of the life of Jesus Christ. His remarkable blueprint for living can forever transform your sense of potential . . . if you let it.

If you have never seriously considered the viability of a personal faith in Jesus Christ, now is the best time to do it. Far beyond his role as a model for life, Jesus came to offer himself as your substitute.

Let me explain. In God's economy, everything has a price. Every decision we make carries the certainty of future consequence. Each time you make a decision to deny your conscience and God's perfect standards—in what you say, think, or do—you accumulate an indebtedness before God. Someday, you will have to pay up.

God calls these decisions against him "sin," and he says those sins have a price. The price is separation from him for eternity. That would have guaranteed you a hopeless future—had it not been for Jesus Christ. When he came to earth, he came to solve your problem before God. He came to take upon himself the penalty for your sins and the sins of all humanity. He came to settle the score with God the Father for you.

On the Cross, God unleashed all of the just penalty for your sins on Jesus. During those agonizing hours of his death, he suffered the full effects of God's justice to make your pardon possible. When he died, the entire settlement for your failure before God was taken care of in Jesus. He paid a debt he didn't owe in order to make you free.

Death. It was your fate. But it became Jesus' choice instead. Three days after his death, he came to life and left the tomb in which he had been buried. He said he had the power to take up his life again, and he did. He said he had the power to forgive your sin and to give you eternal life, and he does. He says he will vouch for you before his Father at the final judgment, and will see to it that you join him for eternity.

But there's something you must do to receive these benefits and enter into a vibrant, living relationship with God. The Bible describes it as accepting Jesus—believing that he is who he claimed to be, that he did what he said he would do, and that he is the only one who can save you from judgment. If you've never made the conscious decision to surrender your life to Jesus Christ, your smartest move is to do it now. You may express these thoughts to him in a simple prayer:

> God, I know I have done things in my life that aren't acceptable to you. I admit those things and ask you to forgive me. I believe that Jesus died to pay the debt for my sins. I believe that he is your son, and that he rose from death and returned to you in heaven. I want to surrender my life to him now, and receive the gift of eternal life. I open my life to your presence. Thank you for loving me enough to die for me on the cross.

If you have expressed this desire to God, you've joined countless millions before you who have entrusted their lives to God's care. You have received a part in God's great purpose for the men and women in his family—a purpose articulated by Jesus just before he returned to heaven:

All power in heaven and on earth is given to me. So go and make followers of all people in the world. Baptize them in the name of the Father and the Son and the Holy Spirit. Teach them to obey everything that I have told you. You can be sure that I will be with you always. I will continue with you until the end of the world.

Those are your marching orders. Join us in the mission. And start now!

A Word About
Priority Living

Bob Shank is the founder and president of Priority Living, an innovative non-profit organization that serves men and women in the business community. He addresses hundreds of company meetings, convention events, conferences, community groups, and Christian audiences each year.

Priority Living focuses on personal development for career-driven people, addressing contemporary issues from the historic Judeo-Christian perspective. Its themes include leadership development, ethics and values, interpersonal relationships, and management skills enhancement.

For information on cassette resources, special seminars and conferences, or to schedule Bob Shank as a speaker for business, community, or church events, contact:

Priority Living, Inc.
17240 East 17th Street, Suite 200
Tustin, California 92680
Telephone: (714) 544-8903

Appendix

One of the challenges facing you at this point is translating the principles and concepts of Total Life Management into your daily approach to life. It often seems that good intentions and great ideas don't end up affecting life on a practical plane due to the lack of systems or tools. Let me introduce you to a resource that will allow you to make your mission-driven life a reality.

As I wrestled myself with the principles of Total Life Management, I found that my daily schedule was a cause for ongoing concern. Most of the things I found myself doing were put into my schedule by someone else, rather than by me. My days were spent responding to other people and their agendas rather than doing what I knew was necessary to pursue my mission. What a sobering realization!

About that time, I discovered a personal planning system that captured my attention. Rather than being a receptacle for an unfocused schedule, it was a tool that enabled me to give clarity to what I was trying to accomplish in life, this year, this quarter, and even today. Here was a means by which my hour-by-hour activities could be tied to the big picture of my life.

The calendar I had been using was no help in solving this problem . . . it was simply allowing me to be organized in doing things that were good, but not best. I've used some kind of personal time system for over fifteen years, but I'd never found anything that addressed the challenge of living a mission-driven life like the Total Life Management DAY-FOCUS™ System.

I'm now hooked. I use the DAY-FOCUS™ System, and it's a winner. It has helped me bring my personal, family, professional, and spiritual dimensions into harmony in the nitty-gritty of my daily schedule. The principles I've learned through Total Life Management are served through the thoughtful planning that now goes into my life commitments.

Maybe the prospect of spending less time and energy to accomplish more of your most important objectives is attractive to you. Perhaps the chance to invest more time in truly important things that may go begging today because of the stressing demands of business is valuable to you. You may be wondering how to really turn the corner from marginal success to personal significance . . . you know you need a process to help make your desires come into being.

DAY-FOCUS™ will assist you in cultivating four personal habits that are foundational for personal success:

Habit #1: Establish clear, written focus.
Habit #2: Plan your week the week before. Plan your day the day before.
Habit #3: Write down every commitment at the time it is made.
Habit #4: Record in one place all action items and follow-up notes for the people and projects you manage.

Denis Waitley, management consultant and best-selling author of *The Psychology of Winning*, says this about the system:

"DAY-FOCUS™ is the first executive organizer ever to make the habits for success a daily part of your personal and professional time management. DAY-FOCUS™ is my secret. I invite you to make it yours."

I'd like to make information about this remarkable system available to you while the principles of Total Life Management are still fresh in your mind. The chances of adopting a mission-driven approach to your life will skyrocket with a resource in your possession to turn your desire into reality.

To receive a free packet explaining The Total Life Management DAY-FOCUS™ System, or to arrange for delivery immediately, mail or phone:

DAY-FOCUS, Inc.
31921 Camino Capistrano, Suite 9104
San Juan Capistrano, CA 92675
Toll-free telephone: (800) 662-5300